Religion & Culture in Africa

A Partial List of Publications by M & J Grand Orbit

1. *Four Decades in the Study of Languages & Linguistics in Nigeria*
2. *In the Linguistic Paradise*
3. *Languages & Culture in Nigeria*
4. *Trends in the Study of Language & Linguistics in Nigeria*
5. *Convergence: English and Nigeria Languages*
6. *Language, Literature and Culture in Nigeria*
7. *Critical Issues in the Study of Linguistics, Languages & Literatures*
8. *Language Policy, Planning & Management in Nigeria*
9. *Language, Literature & Communication in a Dynamic World*
10. *Language, Literature & Culture in a Multilingual Society*
11. *Issues in Contemporary African Linguistics*
12. *Language Endangerment: Globalisation & the Fate of Minority Languages in Nigeria*
13. *Globalization & the Study of Languages in Africa*
14. *Numeral Systems of Nigerian Languages*
15. *The Syntax of Igbo Causatives: A Minimalist Account*
16. *Eleme Phonology*
17. *Basic Linguistics: For Nigerian Language Teachers*
18. *English Studies and National Development*
19. *Language, Literature & Literacy in a Developing Nation*
20. *Language & Economic Reforms in Nigeria*
21. *The Syntax & Semantics of Yorùbá Nominal Expressions*
22. *Functional Categories in Igbo*
23. *Affixation and Auxiliaries in Igbo*
24. *A Grammar of Contemporary Igbo*
25. *A Concise Grammar & Lexicon of Echie*
26. *Bette Ethnography: Theory and Practice*
27. *Topical Issues in Sociolinguistics: The Nigerian Perspective*
28. *Studies in Nigerian Linguistics*
29. *Intercultural Communication & Public Policy in Nigeria*
30. *House of Skulls - A Symbol of Warfare & Diplomacy in Pre-Colonial Niger Delta & Igbo Hinterland*

Readings on
Religion & Culture in Africa

Edited by

Chris I. Ejizu
Professor of Religion
Dept. of Religious & Cultural Studies, University of Port Harcourt, *Nigeria*

M & J Grand Orbit Communications Ltd, Port harcourt

M & J Grand Orbit Publications
Box 237 Uniport P.O., University of Port Harcourt, **Nigeria.**

E-mail: mekuri01@yahoo.com
Mobil Phone: 08033410255, 080333589169

© 2016 M & J Grand Orbit Communications Ltd

All rights reserved. No part of this work may be used or reproduced in any manner without written permission from the Copyright owner.

ISBN 978-978-54208-6-9

Published by

M & J Grand Orbit Communications Ltd., Port Harcourt, **Nigeria.**

Overseas Distributors:

African Books Collective
PO Box 721, Oxford OX1 9EN, United Kingdom
Tel: +44 (0) 1865 58 9756, Fax: +44 (0) 1865 412 341
US Tel: +1 415 644 5108

Customer Services please email
orders@africanbookscollective.com

For Warehouse/shipping/deliveries:
+44 (0) 1865 58 9756

Preface

This is a book of reading on religion and culture in Africa comprising ten (10) well-written papers by experts in religion and cultural matters and an introductory note by the editor himself.

The first paper written by E.S. Akama examines the impact of secularisation and urbanisation on a most cherished socio-cultural practice of the extended family system of the Isoko people in Nigeria.

The second paper written by J.O. Ubrurhe discusses the traditional medical practices in Urhobo with particular focus on the use of local herbs to treat ailments.

The paper by G. Taise and E. Obe discusses the socio-religious as well as the political significance of *Obiri* (family hall) in Ikwerreland.

J. Enowosa explains the rationale behind the use of the concept 'Dunamis' in the Gospel According to Staint Mark. Although his paper does not focus on African (traditional) religion, its inclusion here is based purely on the theological significance of the concept of 'Dunamis'.

Adogbo's paper examines the extent to which evil spirits and mysterious forces have influenced the religion and culture of the Urhobo people of Nigeria. The paper also discusses the problems associated with the belief in these evil spirits and mysterious forces as well as the control mechanism for these unwanted spirits.

Ejizu's paper is on the significance of festivals in the traditional African society.

J.H. Enemugwem discusses John Wesley's innovations in Christendom and their implications for Africa.

A. Kilani frowns at the recent unprecedented upsurge in the assumed use of religious powers to cast out evil spirits as well as for prayer healing among Muslims in Nigeria.

V.G. Nyoyoko discusses the culture of alienation, anxiety and violence, drawing inspiration from the Fall Story of Genesis 3. The rationale behind the inclusion of this paper is due mainly to the significance of the major theme of the paper.

D.I. Ilega discusses an agonising aspect of traditional African culture, which is the widowhood practices in some areas in Nigeria.

This volume is a careful assemblage of well-written papers on different aspects of religion and culture. It is recommended for scholars in religious and cultural studies and those in related areas.

Table of Contents

Preface   v

1. Religion & Culture: An Introduction   1
   -*Chris I. Ejizu*

2. The Impact of Secularization & Urbanization on the Socio-Religious Life of the African Extended Family: The Experience of the Isoko People   5
   -*E.S. Akama*

3. Communicating with Herbs: An Aspect of Urhobo Medicine   25
   -*J.O Ubrurhe*

4. Tradition and Change in the Socio-religious Functions of *Obiri* in Ikwerre   49
   -*George Tasie & Esther Obe*

5. The Use of *Dunamis* in Mark   79
   -*J. Enuwosa*

6. Evaluation of Evil Spirits, Mysterious Forces and the Control Mechanism in Urhoboland   103
   -*M.P. Adogbo*

7. The Meaning & Significance of Festivals in
   Traditional African Culture & Life　　　　　　　121
   　　-Chris I. Ejizu

8. The Innovations of John Wesley in Christendom
   and their Consequences for Africa　　　　　　　153
   　　-John H. Enemugwem

9. Religion, Health & Healing: A Case Study of Prayer
   Healing & Exorcism among Muslims in Nigeria　189
   　　-Abdulrazaq Kilani

10. The Fall Story of Genesis 3: The Experience of the
    Culture of Alienation, Anxiety & Violence　　　221
    　　-Vincent G. Nyoyoko

11. Widowhood Practice in some Southern Nigerian
    Ethnic Groups: An Appraisal　　　　　　　　　249
    　　-Daniel I. Ilega

1. Religion & Culture: An Introduction

Chris I. Ejizu
Dept. of Religious & Cultural Studies, University of Port Harcourt.

Issues of religion and culture relate to questions that are of deep significance to people. They are matters of real concern. Culture is the total way of life of a people, their pattern of family life and social integration, eating habits, manner of greetings, goods, services, fundamental view of reality as a whole, way of structuring power and authority, of adjusting and surviving in the environment, etc. Religion deals with people's beliefs and relationship with spiritual beings. Within that broad frame of reference, religion basically is an aspect of culture. Both religion and culture are intricately interwoven. They mutually interact, and significantly influence each other.

Traditionally, the different groups in Nigeria have been well interested in the affairs of, and relationship with their gods as well as in other aspects of their individual and communal life. Religion plays a preeminent role as it anchors and undergirds the social, political, economic and other aspects of the people's culture. In fact, it has been described as the womb of the culture in the indigenous background of various

Nigerian groups as it imbues, and invests other aspects of life with meaning and significance.

In contemporary society, religion has kept many of its traditional roles, particularly the function of fellowship and communication between humans and the supernatural order, as well as providing explanation and means of control of space-time events to people. But there has also been considerable anxiety over a number of developments. The number and rate of splintering of religions, coupled with the apparent contradiction between statistical growth in numbers, on the one hand, and the crippling moral malaise in society, on the other, are issues of worrying concern. Not only among Christians does the prevailing ambivalence constitute a source of disquiet, Muslims and indigenous religionists equally express concern over the unprecedented religious explosion vis-à-vis the evident indices of decline in the standard of morality in the country.

Culture continues to undergo considerable evolution with mixed fortunes along the way. The period of drawn-out denigration, opposition and bludgeoning by agents of colonialism and misguided missionary religious enthusiasts, has fortunately come to an end. But, the flood of alien cultures, western thought-systems, modern socio-political and economic development has continued to unleash forces of radical change that engulf virtually every aspect of the indigenous cultures. Currently, however, the wind of positive and progressive change and disposition blows. Government and its agencies now appear to appreciate better the significance of indigenous culture in the overall development of both people and economy. Religion and culture are still very much with us. But their features and forms are radically changing in present-day Nigerian society as in several other regions of Africa.

There is the need to up-date our state of knowledge in the two areas. This prompted the compilation of this volume to address matters relating to the twin-subject of religion and culture.

2. The Impact of Secularization & Urbanization on the Socio-Religious Life of the African Extended Family: The Experience of the Isoko People

E.S. Akama
Dept. of Religious & Cultural Studies, University of Port Harcourt.

Introduction

It is now known that Africans, in the past, had their distinct technology, philosophies, concepts, spiritual values and ideas which were fairly sophisticated. Some of these were well-suited to our society and environment (Nwachukwu, 1984:4). Therefore, the way of life of the African peoples is part of their creative intelligence which should be considered as important in the modern scientific and technological age. It is, however, a truism that today most African societies are undergoing a process of rapid and forcible transformation, comparable only to the violent changes of a revolution. This transformation is in diverse ways – socio-economic, political and religio-cultural. Consequently, the traditional systems and institutions have, in most cases, been forcibly wrenched away largely as a result of western "agents of change".

In the light of the foregoing, this paper seeks to present a socio-religious exposition of the place of the extended family and its associated cherished values in our present-day African socio-religious life. Using the experience of the Isoko ethnic group in Nigeria as case-study, the paper examines how this cherished age-old African social institution has now suffered major setbacks today owing to the impact of secularization and urbanization, both of which are potent modern agents of change.

I consider this study significant and relevant for our present age because, as we are being rightly reminded by James Welch, the urge for permanence of things which are worthwhile in a transient world has the creative motive of all great works; it has also given us the sorrow we feel when we look back over the centuries and see what we have lost on the way (Welch, 1931:556). Considering the general African quest for rapid sociological and technological development and modernity, it is hoped that a proper articulation and utilization of the findings in this paper will help to ensure our people a healthy developmental pattern that will take into cognizance the cherished traditional norms and values of our forefathers. This is also significant because the knowledge of the totality of our past, present and future also helps us to determine the true path of our development. It will also help us to revive or redirect some of our cherished social, religious and moral values to the more permanent purpose of our society.

The Structure of a Typical Isoko Family
In the African traditional setting, generally the ethnic group, such as the Isoko of the Delta State of Nigeria, is made up of clans, villages, extended families and nuclear families. The ethnic group generally, has a council of elders or chiefs each representing their clans. Each council is headed by an *Ovie* (King) or *Odiologbo* (Eldest-male) who ascends the throne as a result of either hereditary right or by virtue of age. These monarchs thus have names peculiar to each ethnic group. The monarch or ruler, with his council, exercises authority over the whole ethnic group.

The clans that constitute the ethnic group are made up of villages which are groups of persons closely united by common descent whose head is usually the eldest male member or a king from a recognized royal family of the clan. Like the ethnic group, the clan usually has a clan-head who is either the eldest male of the group or a king as a result of hereditary right. Like the leader or ruler of the ethnic group, the authority of the clan-head and his council of village elders and chiefs is also recognized by all the villages that constitute the clan. The clan may be matrilineal or patrilineal. In some cases, the clan may have a particular plant or animal as a totem. For instance, in Isoko, the Emevor clan has the *Owozo* (Igwana) as its clan totem. The villages that constitute the clan are, in some cases, hierarchically organized according to age-grades which are under the village-head. Each member of the village thus graduates from one age-grade to the other as they grow up. In each case, members are initiated into each age-grade, especially during annual festivals and are taught the laws, duties and rights of the age-group.

The villages are, however, made up of a number of extended families which are in turn made up of nuclear families. The nuclear family, consisting of a man (father) and his wife or wives and children, was the basic unit in native sociology. Socio-economically the nuclear family constituted a basic unit of economic co-operation and social solidarity (Westermann, 1926:422).

The nuclear family is usually linked by close jural and ritual ties to the other similar units through kinship between the respective nuclear family-heads. A number of nuclear families thus form a lineage or extended family that would recognize the authority of the oldest male. In sociological context, the extended family system had to do with the mode of organization of the family and this form of family is made up of the father, mother, children and their relatives. They all live together either in a compound or in several units of houses that are contiguous to one another or in some cases in different localities but bound up by consanguinity. It is usually triple generation in depth (Adesoye, 1988:9). It is on this extended family system this essay is particularly focused.

The Socio-Religious Life of the Isoko Extended Family
Because of the general African belief in the continuous existence of human life and that the deceased ruling elders of the lineage in the spirit world still continually see to the well-being of the living members of their lineages, the Isoko people generally exhibit a very strong proclivity to venerate the deceased ruling elders generally referred to as *esemo* (ancestors). This has led to the erection of lineage ancestral shrines where lineage members, as a duty, occasionally and seasonally meet to offer rituals to the *esemo* (ancestors) and to deliberate on lineage affairs as the need arises. In all cases, the living eldest male of the extended family acts as priest and chief judge. He tries cases and imposes fines on erring members. This forum was thus used for disciplining members and for teaching the basic attitude or spirit of honesty, truth, charity, hospitality, courage, co-operation, respect for elders, sympathy and love was instilled in the members, especially the youths of the lineage. All these virtues were often emphasized by the living ruling elders of the extended families especially when members congregated at the lineage ancestral shrines for rituals and to discuss lineage affairs. Great importance was attached to this because it was generally believed that if the display of these virtues was not extended by any one to a fellow lineage member at one point or the other

would attract the displeasure and wrath of the *esemo* (ancestors).

In the light of the foregoing evidence, to have an ancestral shrine was thus a compelling religious function to a typical Isoko extended family. The extended family thus had significant socio-religious roles to play. It had, among other things, the effect of conditioning the people's religious outlook and behaviour. Traditionally, the upbringing of the children of the nuclear family groups was the concern not only of the parents but of all the adult members of the extended family. Because the extended family is made up of people who are related to each other by blood, the members had a collective image and a common interest especially a name to protect. They were so closely knit in blood that whatever happened to one affected the rest family members. They recognized each other as brothers and sisters. None lived in isolation and in want. The Isoko life at the level of the lineage was therefore predominantly communal. This is characteristic of any typical African traditional community. Against this background of the Isoko strong experience and sense of community that we can appreciate President Kenneth Kaunda's Ujamaa theology and philosophy of Humanism on which Zambia's political philosophy is in turn based. And it has been argued that Kenneth Kaunda who originated this philosophy, made it clear that its success depends on a religious attitude and on a concept of soul as the centre of a network of relationships (Kaunda, 1978:112). It has thus been emphasized that the traditional African family is in many respects the philosophy, theology and ethics of the African Traditional Religion. It is institutionally and practically its fundamental cell. It is the co-agent with the traditional religion in the maintenance of social institutions, social values, public order and morality (Iwe, 1991:3).

Discussing the origin of the extended family system, Dupe Adesioye, quoting T.U.Obviyan, contended that in the African setting, a quest for better adaptation to the environment and the attainment of goals probably led to this type of organization. The argument also has it that the concept of the family originated in Africa and that it was easier to combine and ward off dangers than to allow individuals to cope with the hazardous terrains. In the African system generally the family was the basic integrating instrument. It contained all the functions that make up the totality of society and that in the extended family there was a certain norm which was crucial for its survival and this was the norm of reciprocity; that is, families should exist in a co-operative system in which every member benefits. The argument also has it that this form of reciprocity is highlighted particularly in the area of welfare and that it is on record that the African system does not allow any member to become destitute. One of the fundamental canons is that family members should help their brothers. (Adesoye, 1988:9). As Nassau put it:

> *However successful a man may be in trade, hunting or any other means of gaining wealth, he cannot, even if he would, keep all to himself. He must share with the family whose indolent members thus are supported by the more energetic or industrious. Not only financial rights but all other rights and responsibilities were absorbed by the superior rights and duties of the family* (Nassau, 1904:156).

This observation, no doubt, corroborates Omole's contention that our traditional extended family system epitomizes charity and that our age-old traditional mode of existence is humanist in which communal living makes each citizen his brother's keeper (Omole, 1983:7). Against the background of the foregoing arguments, the extended family can be regarded as the traditional African version of social insurance for old age and welfare for the less-well-to-do members of the society. In it could be seen the functional relationship between religion and social organization. Indeed, the extended family, as the first vital cell of society, was the most cohesive social group, primarily because of the collective image. It is, therefore, not surprising that the observation has been made that before being evangelized and coming into contact with the West, the people of Africa possessed a genuine structure and underlying this structure was a philosophy of life that was not given explicit expression. Also, underlying it was an attitude towards society (Zoa, 1978:76). How this cherished age-old indigenous system is being threatened by the modern forces of change, using Isoko as case study, therefore, attracts our academic attention and investigation.

The Impact of Secularization and Urbanization

For the purpose of clarity, we would like to define the terms 'Secularization' and 'Urbanization'. According to David Edwards, secularization means the displacement from a society's centre of belief in the eternal God, in the 'after-life' as man's great hope and in supernatural force as man's great ally. Edwards also contends that secularization occurs when supernatural religion, that is, religion based on 'belief in God or a future state' becomes private, optional and problematic (Edwards, 1969:16). In the same vein, Edmund Ilogu, in the words of Bryan Wilson, defines secularization as the process whereby religious thinking, practice and institutions lose social significance. In other words, secularization simply means, the organization of man's activities and institutions without reference to religion and the demands of religion. He accentuates:

Before this period in human history, that is, at the end of the 19th century, religious thinking, practice and institutions were of great social significance. Secularization, therefore is a 20th century phenomenon (Ilogu, 1973:12).

The distinction between 'religion' and the 'secular' can be seen in the concepts of 'other-worldliness' and 'this-worldliness' respectively. It is widely supposed that we live in a secular world where the norms of science constantly erode the norms of religion and that religion must adjust to a scientific age if it is to survive. This general supposition is, therefore, gradually affecting man's religious beliefs and practices, the world over.

Urbanization is the process by which a society that was formerly rural becomes thickly populated with modern facilities and industries largely because of modernity and the mass movement of people from different rural communities to urban centers .Urbanization which is closely associated with industrialization is, therefore, part and parcel of the ongoing process of modernization. Secularization and urbanization are, therefore, basic factors of change that affect a people's world-view and life-pattern. Our discussion of the impact of secularization and urbanization here should, however, not to be taken to mean that we are unaware that other agents of change such as Christianity and education do contribute to the ongoing change in Africa. The choice of the two concepts, secularization and urbanization, are just for our working purpose in this essay.

Two broad categories of the impact of secularization and urbanization on the life of a people has been identified – one sociological and the other conceptual. Although there seems to be no strong dichotomy between the two, sociological considerations affect the status of traditional family structure while conceptual considerations arise from new contacts and ideas that produce a new sophistication (Osume, 1988:32). Both of these categories shall be used here for explaining the impact of secularization and urbanization on the extended family life in Africa today, based on our Isoko experience.

Empirical evidence has overwhelmingly shown that there is today a general drift or migration of Isoko youths and able-bodied persons from the rural areas (which are their ancestral homes) to the urban centers or cities such as Warri, Lagos, Port Harcourt which are made up of mixed population. This drift is largely because of economic necessity and the motivation to share in the exciting way of life in the urban centers thus causing the growth of these cities. With time, owing to the unpredictable life in the cities, those who have migrated there from their ancestral homes tend to turn their backs against their extended families to which their umbilical cords are traditionally tied. In the course of development, these migrants would, in their alien abodes, later form a new kind of family which Otite and Ogionwo call "the nuclear organized family", consisting of a man, his wife and their children. This type of family group behaves relatively impersonally and tends to exclude distant or even near Kinsmen (Otite and Ogionwo, 1979:125). This type of urban development eventually causes the decentralization of the old extended family structure; a trend which is now noticeable in many Isoko communities today.

While in the urban area, the urbanite imbibes new ideas and rules or new moral codes and standards of living different from those in vogue in his ancestral home. In other words, he now acquires new ways of life through city influences. He soon becomes ambivalent to the traditional religious life of his kinsmen in the village. It has been truly argued that some migrants in the cities are lured to joining unchristian organizations in order to be influential or to be able to make easy contacts. What some of them would not practise in their own towns and villages they are sometimes forced by circumstances to practise with impunity in the cities (Arulefela, 1987:48-49). Consequently, the urbanite begins to look down on the traditional beliefs and practices of his kinsmen. Soon he begins to brand some of the religious beliefs and practices of his kinsmen as 'barbaric' and 'primitive' and so irrelevant to his needs. This, in many Isoko communities, has led to the weakening or disappearing of lineage ancestral worship. This, in turn has contributed, in no small measure, to the destruction of the extended family system. Thus, it has been observed that the battering of the traditional family structures as well as the acquired radicalism of the youths through their exposure to the forces of modernity and urbanization have affected ancestral worship and moral behaviours (Osume, 1988:36).

Doubtless, the rapid disappearance or weakening of the lineage ancestral worship has affected all the Isoko traditional norms and values associated with it. For instance, the previous collective image and common interest of the extended family that were sustained by this system have broken down because the previous co-operative, communal or the well-farist system associated with it have been lost. Instead, a new urbanized code characterized by individualism and selfishness is gradually evolving. The norms or basic ideas of accountability, sense of belonging, reciprocity and hospitality are also getting lost.

Because of the waning of the ancestral cult in many Isoko communities, lineage affairs are no longer discussed and problems between members are not settled there as before. Instead, such problems are settled in the government law-courts and this has created stress and division in some Isoko lineages today. Discipline in the lineages has also collapsed as the urbanites and the youths no longer respect lineage elders and the rules and regulations which they uphold on behalf of the lineage ancestors. Ancestral laws are, therefore, flouted by the urbanites with impunity because while in the cities they feel emancipated from the authority of the lineage elders. Apparently, because of urban pressure, the urbanite no longer sees himself as his brother's keeper. It is little wonder that Godwin Osuagwu has observed that like their colonial predecessors, the new indigenous technocrats in West Africa, have now taken over the Government Reservation Areas (GRA) where they live in comfort and abundance, insensitive to the troubles of their fellow citizens. Families are beginning to fall apart as a result of urban pressure, individualism, clash of interests and desire for more and more consumer goods (Osuagwu, 1983:14).

Conclusion
Our brief exposition has shown that the impact of secularization and urbanization on the spiritual, religious and moral lives of Africans cannot be overemphasized. Using the Isoko experience generally, as example, we have seen that the urban dwellers who have migrated from the rural communities, for one reason or the other,

often imbibe secularist ideas largely through exposure to urban influences. When they return to the rural areas, such ideas eventually influence the world-view and socio-religious and moral behaviours of the members of their communities especially those of their extended families who now regard the urbanites as role models. Consequently, less and less importance is being placed on the traditional religion especially as practised in the lineage ancestral shrines. The lineage ancestral worship with all its associated norms and values are thus being abandoned. The secularist tendency and the urban influences have therefore, to a large extent, disintegrated the African family and social life. Against this background, it has been argued that in the age of development, the spiritual risk of this trend is very great for as we separate everyday life from religion, we are breaking up the unity and wholeness of life (Omoyajowo, 1978:96). This is the plight of the African extended family system today with all its associated cherished norms and values.

It is my humble submission that in our desperate bid for modernity, materialism or affluence and attempts to be like the Westerner, we need to be careful not to suppress African values associated with the extended family system simply because the West has lost such values with the rise of modern agents of change. Under the euphoria of modernity or civilization, we need not be passive consumers of Western cultural goods and values. We need a civilization that is real and truly African. In this regard, we need to preserve our own traditions in our fast changing world. This is significant because our traditions are supposed to make us whom we are. To this end, the traditional responsibilities and authority of the lineage heads and the ancestral laws which they hold in trust for their forebears need to be preserved. This, no doubt, will contribute to the evolution of our much desired African cultural identity which will be part of our contribution to world civilization. In this regard, the warning of the European missionary, James Welch, who ministered in Isokoland becomes noteworthy that the entry of atomized civilization into a unified African society carries with it the danger of the loss of something far more valuable than anything Western civilization can offer. The African is intensely spiritual; tribal society displays and is held together by a sense of solidarity such that what one man does may and often does affect the whole community. Man is his brother's keeper. Africans know and feel that they are members one of another. These elements are priceless and must be preserved. Westermann concludes that:

> *The African knows more of the true meaning of life and of relations between persons than the individualist Westerner. The enterprise to which we (Christians) are*

called is to seek the truth of human existence in the relations between persons. This is, indeed, the answer to secularism. And in this truth of human existence, the African is the teacher and the European is the learner (Welch, 1931:37).

The foregoing observation of Welch and Westernann is also my song, my prayer and my call on all well-meaning Africans in general and the Isokos in particular, whatever their stations, to help save our age-old extended family system with its cherished norms and values from being totally extirpated from our socio-religious life today.

References

Adesioye, Dupe, "The Extended Family System: Definition", *Sunday Times*, Dec. 11, 1988.

Arulefela, J.O., "Migration and its impact on the Church in Nigeria", *Religions: A Journal of the Nigerian Association of the Study of Religions*, 12:1, 1987.

Edwards, L. David, *Religion and Change*, London: Hodder and Stoughton, 1969.

Ilogu, E., "The Influence of Christianity on Education in this Age of Secularization", *The Nigerian Christian*, Vol. 8, No. 3, March 1973.

Iwe, N.S.S, "Sociological Approach to the Study of the African Traditional Religion and Culture" (Paper presented at the 6th Annual Conference of the National Association of African Religion and Culture, University of Port Harcourt), 2 – May, 1991.

Kaunda, Kenneth, "Spirituality and World Community", *African Christian Spirituality*, Shorter, A.W.F. (ed.), London: Rex Collings Ltd., 1978.

Nassau, R.H., *Fetishims in West Africa*, London: Duckworth and Co., 1904.

Nwachukwu, Ike, "Re-assessing Cultural Intellectual Growth of Our Ancestors" (Imo State Military Governor's Address Delivered at the 1984 Ahiajaku Lectures in Owerri), *Sunday Statesman*, Sunday Dec. 9, 1984.

Omole, A.A., "Task of Adjusting to Ethical Revolution", *Daily Times*, Tuesday Feb. 22, 1983.

Omoyajowo, J. Akin, "Christianity as a Unifying Factor in a Developing Country", *African Christian Spirituality*, Shorter, A.W.F (ed.) London: Rex Collings Ltd, 1978.

Osuagwu, Godwin U., "Impact of Westernization on West African Institutions: A Socio-Political Analysis" (A paper presented at the Second Annual Social Science Colloqium, University of Texas), *Sunday Statesman*, Oct 2., 1983.

Osume, C.E., "The Impact of Development on Okpe Traditional Religion", *Journal of the Nigerian Association for the Study of Religions* (N.A.S.R), Dopamu, Ade P. (ed.) 1988.

Otite, Onigu and Ogionwo, W., *An Introduction to Sociological Studies*, Ibadan: Heinemann Educational Books (Nig. Ltd), 1979.

Welch, J.W. "An African Tribe in Transition", *The International Review of Missions*, Vol.3, London: Oxford University Press, 1931.

Westermann, D., "The Values of the African Past" *The International Review of Missions*, Vol. 3, London: Oxford University Press, 1931.

Zoa, John, "Christian Commitment in African", *African Christian Spirituality*, Shorter, A.W.F. (ed.) London: Rex Collings Ltd., 1978.

3. Communicating with Herbs: An Aspect of Urhobo Medicine

J.O Ubrurhe
Department of Religious Studies, Delta State University, Abraka

> *Self–preservation is a fundamental instinctive tendency of all organisms. Consequently every organism-human, animals and including plants –adopts some kind of activity meant to perpetuate itself, to protect itself from harm when threatened and to activate any part that is temporarily affected by some disability* (Ejizu 1987:18.).

Introduction

Self-preservation is a basic innate tendency of all organisms. In every culture there is, therefore, an indigenous medical system, which preserves, enhances and sustains life whenever it diminishes into a state of disease and affliction. This medical system is often designated traditional. The adoption of this designation emanated from the fact that the medical system was practiced by the progenitors and later bequeathed to their progeny. The transmission of this cultural heritage is usually done orally and through practice. The ubiquity of this genre of medical system is responsible for some scholars' argument that orthodox medicine is the summation of human medical heritage from diverse cultures, nationalities and race.[2]

The existence of this medical system in every culture presupposes that there are bound to be areas of continuity and discontinuity. These points of similarity and difference do not in any way mitigate the efficacy of the medical system or do they make one superior to the other. It is, however, noteworthy that some of these varied traditional medical systems have been improved upon from time to time to the point of attaining international acceptability, such as the Chinese acupuncture.

The focus of the paper is on Urhobo medicine, a medical system which was practised by the Urhobo ancestors and later bequeathed to their descendants. The paper examines a very significant aspect of the system: how the medical practitioner in the process of collecting, preparing and administering of remedies, communicates with the medicinal plants in order to ensure the efficacy of the recipe. Attempt will be made to discuss briefly the Urhobo world-view, the medical practitioners, etiology in Urhobo medicine and their modes of treatment. In the process, the potency of the "word" will of necessity be emphasized since most of the communication is done through words of intention or incantations.

Before the advent of orthodox medicine to Urhoboland, there was never any doubt about the efficacy of Urhobo medicine. Thus, it was the only available medical system, which catered for all forms of disease, misfortune and affliction. In spite of the presence of orthodox medicine in the area, the practice of Urhobo medicine has persisted, waxing stronger and even bestriding orthodox medicine in the rural areas where orthodox medical facilities and personnel are rarely available.

The Urhobo world-view includes the belief in Oghene (God) who is the creator of both animate and inanimate objects. These objects are imbued with life force, which is the quintessence of the object itself. This life force is dormant until it is activated through the use of the word. These objects include the edjo and erha (divinities), irhi (spirits), ohwo (man) eravwe (animals), irhe (trees), irhie (rivers) among others. The Urhobo also believe that Oghene created two worlds; *akpo* (the physical) and *Akpo ra mre–e* (the psychic). These worlds correspond to the visible and invisible or the social and the spiritual realms of existence.

In all their endeavours, the people solicit the assistance of the spiritual realities to ensure success. These endeavours include farming, fishing, business, marriage and medicine-making to mention a few. The universe is basically good with the great forces constantly at work struggling to maintain a greater unity of all the forms. Man/ woman can only achieve what he/she is desirous of, if he/she co-operates with these forces. It is against this backdrop that in Urhobo (Africa) man/woman does not find fulfilment as an individual but one who participates in a family and community. The ontological emphasis in Urhobo world of social values is in consequence of an attempt to maintain good relationship between God and man/woman and other elements in the universe. Significantly Mbiti's statement that "I am because we are, and since we are, therefore, I am" summarizes the Urhobo conception of relationships.

Troubles of various magnitude are associated with collapse in human relationships and yet the preservation and restoration of these relationships are basically important for man's/woman's well-being. There is, therefore, a symbiotic relationship between the spiritual realities and man/woman, which concretizes in the act of worship in which each party has to fulfil his/her own obligation. The failure of man/woman to fulfil his/her own duties creates an imbalance in his/her total well-being which consequently leads to disorientation if appropriate step is not taken in time to remedy it. This disorientation might be physical, psychological or spiritual. Thus the state of well –being or wholeness in the Urhobo context comprehends more than mere physical fitness but wholeness as experienced in the rapport with nature, psychic and social integration in the cosmic forces and the level of human morality.[3]

The Urhobo man/woman on the other hand would also expect his object of worship to fulfil and perform its duties. Where it fails to perform, he/she does not hesitate to abandon or even throw or burn its object of worship for its inability to adhere to the stipulations of the covert covenant. This was one of the main reasons, according to S.U Erivwo, which accounts for the bumper harvest Christianity had when it was first introduced into Urhoboland.[4]

The aetology in Urhobo medicine is fundamentally of three dimensions. These are natural, mystical and supernatural causative factors. Naturally caused diseases respond quickly to treatment. Such diseases include: headache, sore, bellyache, measles, malaria among others. Their treatment involves medicine, which can be analyzed in the Laboratory, and their active ingredients discovered. Their causes depend on cause -effect theory.

Mystical and supernatural diseases are usually serious, exotic and protracted. In most cases they are refractory to the whole gamut of proven therapy. However natural diseases can become serious and protracted through their agencies. These agencies include witches, sorcerers, evil eye, ancestors and divinities. These diseases arise as a result of breakdown in filial relationship for failing to perform one's obligation to the ancestors and divinities; or they may arise as a result of evil eye, jealousy, hatred etc. In both mystical and supernatural diseases, the treatment involves rituals including sacrifice. The focus of this paper, therefore, is on both mystical and supernatural treatment including life enhancement through mystically prepared recipes.

The praxis of Urhobo medicine is within the domain of three specialists: *Ọbọ* (medicine man/woman) *Ọbọepha* (diviner) and *Orherẹ* (priest). They include both men and women. Women in most cases, specialize in obstetrics, gynecology, pediatrics, circumcision of girls and other general treatment while their male counterparts handle special cases of the treatment of leprosy, abscess, gonorrhea among others.[5]

Each of these specialists has his/her distinctive role to perform in the medical system. The Urhobo perception of the aetiology in medicine underscores the role of each specialist. The *ọbọ* heals essentially through the utilization of medicine; the *ọbọepha* through divination while the *Orherẹ* handles diseases emanating from guilt against the gods, ancestors and humanity, which involve offering of sacrifice. Hence Ezeanya contends that the priest is mainly responsible for the performance of sacrifice arising from abominable offences committed against the supersensible realities and man/woman. He considers "a person who has committed an abominable act detestable to the divinities and men/women as really a sick person.[6]

These specialists, men/women of hidden supernatural power, possess esoteric knowledge, which they derived from their training, revelation made by the ancestors, or spirits, while others may acquire it from their fathers or ancestors, or relations who were medicine men/women. Maclean,[7] Prince,[8] Mume[9] among other scholars have asserted that medicine men/women usually come from families with long medical tradition. Such families, they opine, form the contemporary product of traditional lore. The effectiveness and prestige of the medicine man/woman and the efficacy of his/her remedies determine his/her rate of patronage. In Urhobo medicine there is high correlation between efficacy and medicine revealed in dream and by spirits.

During my doctoral fieldwork, many of such stories were narrated to me. I will illustrate with one Mr. E.Okpukoro narrated. He told a story of how a palm branch pricked and stuck in his father's (a palm collector's) leg. All efforts to remove it were to no avail. The leg became swollen and septic to the extent they were despondent and contemplating amputating it. In their desperation, his grandfather who was a medicine man before he died, showed his father the medicine to remove the thorn in a dream. That in the same night, his grandfather also showed the same medicine to his mother in a dream; emphasizing that he (grandfather) knew that his son was forgetful. When the medicine was applied on the leg, the thorn came out on its own. This is an example of Urhobo medicine with occultic power of removing thorns, bullets, injection needles from the body without surgical operation. [10] Initially I was sceptical about the story. I was, therefore, moved to also interview the mother. The mother's story corroborated her son's in every detail.

Methods of Communication while Harvesting Herbs
In Urhobo medicine, there is communication between medical practitioner and the herbs, which he/she collects, prepares and administers as medicament. African communication modes have been put into three broad categories. These include:

(i)   The verbal mode;
(ii) The Non-verbal, and
(iii) The Esoteric/psychomythical mode.

The verbal mode employs the mouth and the spoken words. These include spoken language (dialogue/conversation, etc.), stories (foundation stories, collective memory, pseudo stories, counter stories, Folk Tale or Fable).

The non-verbal mode employs body language (various movements of the body or part thereof to convey meaning), symbolography (arrangements of artifact to express meaning), dance (a special case of body movement) and music (involving technical arrangement of word), song (melody and harmony).

The esoteric/psychomythical mode involves interpretation of dreams, divination, telepathy, rituals and miscellaneous interpretation of nature.[11] In this paper, the verbal and esoteric/psychomythical modes of communication will be examined.

For a better understanding of the communication process, it is important to comprehend the concept of vital force or dynamism in nature. The earth is a reality, which possesses psychic force, energy or dynamism.

Smith defines dynamism as "the belief in and practices associated with hidden, mysterious, supersensible, pervading energy, powers, potencies and forces.[12] Dynamism is dormant and neutral but could be tapped by medicine men/women sorcerers, witches and anybody who cares to possess extra human power. This force is accessible to the initiated through their training and occultic practices. Dynamism is believed to direct medicine men/women to know the herbs to pluck for each type of disease. Oftentimes medicine men/women speak to each herb by appealing to the life force in it. In pursuance of the above argument, Imasogie asserts that dynamism incarnates herbs for the purpose of helping the medicine men/women to obtain therapeutic success. [13]

It is, however, necessary to draw a clear distinction between this vital force and the inherent life force, which the Urhobo and Africans in general believe, the creator has imbued every animate and inanimate objects with. Dynamism does not embody itself in any animate or inanimate object. It is a genre of force in the universe. It is believed to be a dimension in the earth. This is why any person who wants to use it could acquire it through initiation to the appropriate cult. Hence a medicine man/woman who acquired it through his/her training could be directed by it to the appropriate herbs with the appropriate life force capable of effecting cure of such disease.

In the collection of herbs or parts of trees the medicine man/woman usually utters some incantatory evocation by calling the proper name of the herb and making his/her intention known to it. In the case of herbs or trees with high potent life force the modes of communication are both verbal and esoteric/psychomythical. Apart from the incantatory evocation, some sacrifice or offering is usually performed.

My interview with some medicine-men/women revealed that *Akpobrisi* is an example of a tree with very high potent life force. Before collecting any part of it, the medicine man/woman has to pull all his/her dresses a little distance from the tree; and goes nude to it. The medicine man/woman offers some sacrifice, which usually consists of mashed yam mixed with oil and some coins or cowries. The medicine man/woman communicates what he/she wants to do and the purpose of collecting the parts and pleads with the supersensible realities to attend the recipe with effectiveness. Thereafter he/she hits the tree with a club he/she has brought with him/her. A positive response from the tree is indicated by an unusual noise, which vibrates upwards

The medicine man/woman hurriedly collects the parts and run away before the vibration descends. Mysterious stories of how some medicine men/women were killed at the trunk and a few meters from the tree were told. The purpose of pulling the clothes is to make it impossible for the life force to identify the person after he/she had worn his clothes. Any recipe with the part of the trees is usually very effective and always used for the treatment of mystical/supernatural diseases and for the enhancement of life.

It must be emphasized that during the communication with the herbs/trees, the medicine man/woman calls the proper name of the trees preceded by the utterance of words of power which form a large and significant part of Urhobo medicine. For a name is believed to be audible description of the internal forces within a person or thing. The soul, spirit double and name are all integral parts of man's being.[14] In the collection, preparation and administration of medicament for mystical and supernatural diseases and for life enhancement, the proper names of the herbs and patients are in most parts called. This is because of the Urhobo belief that a name is the descriptive vocalization of the unseen latent forces in man, plant or object. These latent forces are activated through incantatory evocation by the initiate. Thus names are significantly the verbalization of the abstract inner qualities of the vital elements inherent in the herbs.

Perhaps it might be necessary to attempt a critical analysis of the potency of *Ota* (Word). *Ota* is the spoken word which possesses mystical power and when recited or chanted either on objects or alone, produces mystical effect.

The animate and inanimate objects in the universe are categorized into four, viz.: Muntu (man), Kintu (thing), Bantu (place and time), and Kintu (modality). Muntu consists of God, all humans and spirits. Kintu includes other animate and inanimate objects in which life forces are dormant and can be activated by a Muntu by the use of the word. They are at the beckon and call of man[15]. The Kintu forces are not self-willed because they lack intelligence, which differentiates them from man. Once stimulated into action the Kintu can on their own influence other beings including man. Man differs from animal because of the word and one man from another because of the relative utilization of the word. Hence the

Urhobo say *Ota oye Ohwo* (it is the word that differentiate one man from the other or the word is a man). *Ota runu Uhuvwu* (the spoken word is the medicine without it there is no medicine).

In Urhobo medicine, the life force inherent in both animate and inanimate objects are activated by the use of *Ota* recited or chanted over them. Hence Janheinz Jahn asserts that "… The word holds the course of things in train and changes and transforms them"[16]. Man is imbued with intelligence and the power of the word, which he exerts on other beings around him. He, therefore, employs them as means to an end. The medicine man/woman harnesses these forces when he/she collects the materia medica, prepares and administers his/her medicine.

The significance of the "word" in the Genesis creation story is summarized in Iwu's words:

> *The word is before every other thing, in its fluid form, it forms the material that fills the oceans and sacred rivers and also provides the soluble base for animal erythrocytes, including those of man.... The word in its simplest concept is a force effective and yet dormant until uttered*[17].

The Book of Genesis and the fourth Gospel (St. John) are positive in their testimony to the creative power of the uttered word. According to Genesis 1:3 "… God said, Let there be light, and there was light' while St. John's Gospel emphasises the pre-existence and creative power of the word "In the beginning was the Word, and the Word was with God " All things were made by him and without him was not anything made that was made" (1:1-3), This, no doubt, was a climatic echo of the mystical testimony to the potency of the spoken word.

Victor Hugo, in the same way, discussed the word and its working in one of the poems of contemplation. He contends that:

> *Il esr vie, espirit, germe, ouragon, vert, feu; car le mot, C' est le verbe, est le verbe, est Dieu.*

> It (word) is life, spirit, germ, hurricane, virtue and fire. For name is the word, and the Word is God.[18]

The Biblical concept of the potency of the word has linkage with the Urhobo belief. In Urhobo medicine the word activates the dormant life force in the herbs and thus makes it efficacious.

Impregnating the Herbs with potency during Preparation and Administration

Communication with herbs usually occurs not only during collection but also during preparation and administration. During the collection the communication is essentially an appeal to the herb to permit the medicine man/woman to collect the necessary parts. He/she also communicates what he/she intends to do with the parts and pleads for the efficacy of the medication. The mode of communication involves calling the proper names of the herbs, offering of libation, sacrifice and in some cases money or cowries are offered at the trunk or foot of the tree/herb.

In the preparation and administration, words of intention or incantations are employed to activate the dormant life force in the herbs. This is mostly done in medication for treating mystically and supernaturally caused diseases and mystical preparation and administration of recipe for life enhancement and achievement of one's aspiration. In Useki (medicine for attracting customers), the potency of the word is evidently indicated.

Materia Medica – iku (crayfish), irhibo evwiewie ighre (seven small peppers) and water.

Preparation - squeeze all items in the water while saying the following incantation:

Eji ineki me bu none na
Kere iku kugbe irhibo evwievwie
Let my customers be as many today
As crayfish and small peppers

Administration – Bathe with the water before going for sales while reciting the above incantation.

Preter-rational treatment performs the above function because it is based on the principles of similarity, contagion and transferability. Similarity is not only limited to the action but also to the individual material which makes up the recipe and is impregnated with the potency of the words of intention (incantations) which explicitly indicates the purpose and power of the resultant mixture.

In the above recipe, crayfish and small pepper are usually many and water is uncountable noun. These materials are similar to the many customers the user of the recipe wants. The incantation "Let my customers be as many as crayfish and small pepper" clearly demonstrates the purpose and the expected power of the resultant recipe.

Another recipe is the medicine for Udidi (awe) and prevention against witches and evil eyes.

Materia medica – Seven young leaves of Uloho (iroko tree), a dry head of obi (cobra), one seed of erhie (alligator pepper), firewood with fire and a bucket of water.

Preparation - Put all items except the firewood, inside the bucket of water, squeeze the leaves and the head of the cobra together. Later put the stick with fire while impregnating the recipe with potency by saying the following incantation:

> *Udid r' Obi oje mue obi-I*
> *Ame boroboro yo furhie erhare*

> Nobody can hold the cobra because of its awe
> Even if water is insipid, it extinguishes fire.

Administration - Use concoction to bathe while reciting the above incantatory evocation.[19]

In this recipe the awe of the cobra and the *iroko* tree are transferred to the user of the medicine. The quality of water in extinguishing fire, even if hot, boiling or cold is also transfer to the user. This will enable the user to command respect and have awe among his colleagues. The power of names in the performance of ceremonies especially magical medicine - their preparation and administration are accompanied by the evocation of words of intention form a large and significant aspect of Urhobo medicine.

In preter-rational medicine and treatment there is intimate relationship between medicine and religion. This has caused confusion between Urhobo and orthodox medical systems. For in orthodox medicine the belief is that it follows natural laws while Urhobo medicine follows both natural and the supernatural laws. This interpenetration of religion in traditional medicine is a fundamental point of departure from orthodox medicine. Religion basically opposes magic and science since the essential assumption of religion is that the course of nature and human life are controlled by spiritual realities superior to man while science exerts mechanical control over nature; magic seeks to force the hands of such beings by bending nature to its wishes through the use of spell and enchantments. Religion courts the favor of such beings through prayer and offering. However when magic fails, persuasion becomes a better alternative. Hence magic is often described as the predecessor of religion.[20]

Conclusion
The aetiological theory in Urhobo medicine identifies three factors natural, mystical and supernatural diseases and its nosology corresponds with the three causal factors. The treatment of natural disease involves the combination of the various forces in the materia medica. This combination sets in motion a chain reaction like in

the natural science. The treatment is usually described as rational.

The treatment of mystical and supernatural diseases and the preparation and administration of recipes for the enhancement of life is often describe as magi co-rational. It is magical because the herbs are impregnated with the potency of the spoken word. It is rational because some of the materials contain active principles, which could effect the cure. The efficacy of such recipes is predicated on the principle of similarity not only the action but also of the material, contagion and transferability. These principles are based on the belief that both animate and inanimate objects possess corporeal and incorporeal existence. The corporeal existence is tangible while the incorporeal is intangible and incorporated in the corporeal. The incorporeal can however be activated or effectuated by the potency of the word, which accompanies the collection, preparation and administration of the medicine.

In Urhobo medicine there is communication between the medical practitioner and the herbs. The modes of communication are both verbs and esoteric/psycho mythical. The purpose of this communication is to enable the medical practitioner to make his/her intention known, what he/she wants to use the herb for and to appeal to the supernatural realities to effectuate the treatment. The verbal mode of communication impregnates the recipe with the potency of the spoken word. To the Urhobo any medicine or recipe in which there is no communication between the medical practitioner, the herbs and the spiritual realities is usually considered inefficacious. Communication in Urhobo medicine is one-dimensional. It is the medicine man that only communicates without a vocalized response from the herbs. However positive response from the herb may be indicated by the efficacy of the recipe while negative response may be portrayed by the ineffectiveness of the medicament. Such communication is a catharsis for the patient. This cathartic situation plays important role in the treatment of psychosomatic or spiritual diseases. Hence it is asserted that Urhobo medical system takes care of the various levels of the awareness of the patient.

Notes and References

1. C.I. Ejizu, *"Healing as Wholeness: The Igbo Experience"* in Africana Marburgensia, Vol. 20, No. 1, (1987) p. 8.
2. M.M. Iwu, *Traditional Igbo Medicine Report of a Project sponsored by the Institute of African Studies, University of Nigeria, Nsukka (1981)*, p. 9.
3. C.I. Ejizu, Opus Cita. p. 13.
4. S.U. Erivwo *Traditional Religion and Christianity in Nigeria: The Urhobo People* (Ekpoma: Dept. of Religious Studies and Philosophy. (1991)
5. J.S. Mbiti *African Religions and Philosophy*, (London: Heinemann, (1973), 157. Also see J.O Kokwora, Medicinal Plants in East Africa, (Nairobi: East African Literature Bureau, (1976), p. 4.
6. S.N. Ezeanya, *"Healing in Traditional African Society0"* in WAR, vol. 17, No. 1 (1978), p. 6.
7. U. Maclean, *Magical Medicine: A Nigerian Case Study*, (London: Reading and Fakenham, (1971), p. 75.
8. R. Prince, *"Some Notes on Yoruba Native Doctors & Their Management of mental illness"* in Conference Report 1st Pan African Psychiatric Conference, Abeokuta, Nigeria, p. 70.
9. J.O Mume, *Traditional Medicine in Nigeria:* (Agbarho: JOM Nature Cure Centre (n.d), p. 1.
10. J.O. Ubrurhe, *"Urhobo Traditional Medicine"* (Ibadan: Spectrum Books, 2003) p. 79.

11. B. Folarin, Dept. of Mass Communication, Delta State University, Abraka Citing G. Mythen, *Mass Commnunication in Africa*, (London: Edward Arnold, 1989).
12. Edwin W. Smith, *African Ideas of God*, cited by E.G. Parrinder, *African Traditional Religion*, (London: Sheldon Press, 1975). p. 21.
13. O. Imasogie, *African Traditional Religion*, (Ibadan: Ibadan University Press, (1985), p. 49.
14. J.A.A. Ayoade, *"The Conception of Inner: Essence in Yoruba Traditional Medicine"* in African Therapeutic Systems, (eds.) Z.A Ademuwagun et.al. (Massachusetts: Crossroad Press, (1979), 51.
15. J.A.A. Ayoade, *Muntu: An Outline of the New Africa Culture,* (New York: Graove Press, (1961), p. 100.
16. Ibid., 133.
17. M.M. Iwu, *"Symbolism and Selectivity in Traditional African Medicine"* A lecture delivered by the winner of vice-Chancellor's Research Leadership Prize for 1987, University of Nigeria, Nsuka, Jan. 12, 1989, p. 10.
18. Cited by Babatunde Folarin, *"The Potency of the spoken word, The Primacy of Oral Communication, and the Implications for Broadcasting in Africa"* A paper first prepared for the ACCE International Conference in memory of Prof. Frank Okwu Ugboajah, Former Head of the Dept. of Mass Communication, University of Lagos, Nigeria; a

founding member of ACCE; and a Leading exponent of "Oromedia", April 24-26 1996. p. 3.
19. Interview with Pa. Eyitemi 21-5-93, Age 85.
20. J.A.A. Ayoade, Op. Cit., p. 50.

4. Tradition and Change in the Socio-Religious Functions of *Obiri* in Ikwerre

George Tasie & Esther Obe
Dept. of Religious & Cultural Studies, University of Port Harcourt.

Introduction

One remarkable thing that will strike a visitor to Ikwerreland[1] is the presence of *Obiri* (family hall) in almost every homestead. *Obiri* is particularly important not only on issues bothering on the people's indigenous religion, but also in Ikwerre settlement patterns, in social, political and economic relations and in scheduling of daily life. But despite its prominence in the socio-religious life of the Ikwerre, *Obiri* has been an object of little scholarly attention. Its only mention in literature was that of P.A. Talbot (1928) who simply described it as the "palaver house of the compound"[2]

Our aim in the present paper is to attempt to demonstrate how in the traditional Ikwerre world a good understanding of the *Obiri* institution is an important gate-way into Ikwerre thought-form, spiritual values and world–view. This paper, therefore, is at once both an interpretation of the role of *Obiri* and an appreciation of its importance as a cohesive factor in Ikwerre traditional society.

The Origin of *Obiri*

The Ikwerre seem to have no definite account on the origin of *Obiri*. Most of what exist are no more than conjectures put forward by elders and opinion leaders. One of such is a popular account which runs as follows: The earliest forebears of the Ikwerre first lived in a house of two rooms. The rooms were commonly known as *oromati* and *orokpobiri*. The former served a dual purpose. First, as the sleeping chamber of the man who was the head of the house and secondly, as a place where he enshrined his *chi* (the deity most closely associated with the existence and fortunes of the individual person) and other patron deities. The latter served as a place of rest; a room for the reception of visitors; a place where family meetings and religious activities involving the group were held; and also served other miscellaneous purposes.

However, as society became more complex, with increase in human relationship and interaction, there arose the need for privacy. This gave rise to the construction of *obokoro*, an outpost building, which was quite detached from the main family house. The idea of *obokoro*, beside solving the immediate problem created by hosting all manner of visitors in the living house, might also have arisen from the fact that not all visitors were friendly. Thus, there was need to remove the prying eyes of enemies from the household. Equally important, was the fact that there were times when the head of the house would not want his family members – wives and children – to hear whatever important discussion he might be holding with his visitors. Examples of such discussions were those that bordered on crucial issues like war, murder and abomination. Such discussions were carried out in the *obokoro* far from the ear-shot of women and children. Similarly, like the *orokpobiri*, *obokoro* served miscellaneous functions; as a place of rest, where folktales were told; and where during harvest season, the family gathered to roast maize, cocoyam and yam. Most importantly, *obokoro* gradually became for the extended family, a centre of religious activities, as important rituals were carried out there.

However, with the family head achieving high social status, more often reflected in acquiring many wives, children and domestic slaves, there arose the need for a large and dignifying out post building which became known as *Obiri* (family hall). The era of slave trade witnessed the addition of yet another small hut erected very close to the entrance of the compound where the slaves were kept. The security implication of this, in the event of any intrusion, was for the slaves to begin first to ward off the attackers before the rest of the household got alerted and joined.[3]

Thus, it seems that the initial idea of *Obiri* was that of accomplishment, wealth and affuence; as it conferred respect on the family head by his neighbours, since only a few could scarcely afford such grandeur.

Another account, however, claim that *Obiri* came into being with the simple reason that the living-room of the head of the family was not wide enough to accommodate his kinsmen whenever there was need for them to assemble in his homestead to discuss important issues concerning the entire family or lineage group. As a result, there arose the need to erect an out post building whose primary duty was to provide accommodation for such impotent lineage meetings.[4] To yet others, the need for *Obiri* arose out of the need for a place for the reception or hosting of visitors[5]

If these views are anything to go by then the role of *Obiri* initially was primarily that of a reception hall where the head of the family received and entertained visitors. Whichever account may be the origin of *Obiri*, it is certain that *Obiri* was quite distinct from *obokoro* (small hut) and not as common as the latter. Gradually, as we shall see in what follows, *Obiri* began to assume a very prominent role in the religious and socio-political life of the Ikwerre, so that by the eve of colonial rule and arrival of Christianity, it had become not only a centre of religious ceremonies and rituals but also a formidable centre for socio-politcal activities.

Location, Social Organization and Distribution

In most Ikwerre homesteads *Obiri* was located either at the centre of the compound or somewhere near the entrance; so that as one entered the homestead, he was immediately confronted by the *Obiri*. In a typical Ikwerre fashion, Talbot describes the location of the *Obiri* in the homestead. Thus; according to him,

> *A typical Ikwerre compound usually is surrounded by a rectangular mud wall (**nbidi**) its front broken by a porched entrance popularly known as **onu usaw** (i.e. mouth of road) leading on to the main thorough fare. Inside, facing the entrance, is an open shade (**Obiri or onu Obiri**) which is raised by the head of the family in token of assuming that position. This forms the general meeting place and palaver house of the compound, and plays an important role in the life of the community.*[6]

Thus, Ikwerre village-groups, in a sense, were characterized by several levels of socio-political organizations. Each compound was inhabited by a single family with the father as head exercising a strong measure of authority over it. Several extended families made up a lineage; several lineages made up a village; and several villages made up the village-group. In this way, there was the level of the simple or compound family; that of the extended family; that of the minor lineage and that of the major lineage. Each was more in power and authority than the one before it. Now for each of these levels of organization, at least, there was a corresponding level of *Obiri*. Thus for each extended family there was an *Obiri* for its common patrilineal ancestor, and so on up to the level of the major lineage. Thus, as an extended family grew into a minor lineage its *Obiri* would have become a minor lineage *Obiri*. Meanwhile, its component families would have become extended families and as such would have acquired their own *Obiri*. So also for minor lineage growing into major lineage. The result was a system of *Obiri*, which in a sense, mirrored the patrilineal socio – political organization of the village. The overall picture was a hierarchy of *Obiri* with unequal status and power which reflected the socio-political structure.

Construction of *Obiri*

When a man was of age, which among the Ikwerre was when he married and left his father's homestead, to set up his own, then there was need for him to erect *Obiri* in his homestead. The man would then approach the eldest man of his patrilineage who might also be the *Owhor* holder (political and religious head) of the lineage with a bottle of locally distilled gin. With this he would tell him of his intention to erect *Obiri* in his homestead. He might also through the *Owhor* holder, solicit the support of the lineage members in executing this task. The *Owhor* holder inturn informed members of the lineage. On the appointed day, the male members of the lineage gather in the homestead of the man who wants *Obiri* to be built in his homestead. They were expected to bring along with them such items as bamboo poles, thatches, livesticks such as *ikeni* and *aja*, which were believed to remain alive for a considerable long period of time.

Before the construction proper commences the *Owhor* holder stands before the proposed site and with a drink in hand libates to *Ali* (the earth deity), the ancestors and other notable deities of the lineage; informing them that one of their own wants to erect an *Obiri* where he would not only rest with his family and entertain guests but also where he would perform some of his religious activities. His prayer run thus:

Ali bia onworu may	Earth deity come and drink
Ele ndayi laru alah	Our departed fathers (ancestors)
Anu bia onworu maya	Come and drink wine
Agbara dum zi ichiche	All manner of deities
Anu bia onworu maya	Come and drink wine
Thah otu nwo anu	Today one of your sons
Choru wute Obiri nu eziah	Wants to erect *obiri* in his homestead.
Osukwuru ayi	He has called us together

Bia eyi nuah akah	To assist him
Obu nu ezi si nu nnadi	It is true that a kinsman
Je azi nu oru aru omu ndaah	Does not labour while his kinsmen
Nu ele ah	watch
Ke kpayaru ayi ijiri bia	Hence we have come
eyi shi nuah akah	to assist him
Ayi yi shi nuah akah	As we assist him let
agbara ojor madu ojor	no malevolent spirit or evil one
Whu ya ayi	Notice us
Oza he ojor dagi de ayi	Let no harm befall us
Nu otu obu ayi je oru	In one accord we shall accomplish
pu aru ah	this task.
Omu nnadi obula ayi kweru kotaru	kinsmen, is that not what we have agreed?
Obu yaah!	Yes! It is[7].

After the prayer, the young men commenced the construction of the *Obiri*; while the elders would sit helping themselves to the drink provided by the young man in whose homestead the *Obiri* was being constructed. The size of *Obiri* varied according to the choice and means of the owner. However, an average *Obiri* was about 15ft. high, 10ft. wide and 18ft. long. *Obiri* was constructed with strong livesticks, bamboo poles and thatches. It was usually raised and supported by two prominent sticks; one at the front and the other at the rear. They were flanked at both ends by one stick each of a smaller size and then by the sides by about two sticks each. It was so built that the front and rear views of the *Obiri* were higher than both sides, which sloped downwards.

When the task of construction was accomplished, the man on whose behalf the kinsmen had gathered to work would feed the lineage members. He would feed them with pounded yam and plenty of palm wine. Afterwards they might depart happily to their homes because their task had been accomplished.

But it is remarkable to note that the man on whose behalf the *Obiri* was built might not put it into use until it was consecrated. To do this the *Owhor* holder was once more invited to perform the rite of consecrating the *Obiri*. The owner of the *Obiri* was expected to acquire a livestock, probably cock or goat as his means might permit. The livestock was brought before the *Owhor* holder who stood at the main entrance into the *Obiri* popularly known as *Onu Obiri* (*Onu Obiri* as we shall see shortly was symbolic in many respects) with a glass of locally distilled gin. He would then libate to the earth deity, the ancestors and other patron deities of the kingroup begging them to always make their presence felt in the *Obiri* at all times so that whatever curse or blessing that is sealed in the *Obiri* becomes binding on those concerned. In the course of the libation he would say:

Ali bia onworu maya	The earth deity come and drink wine
Ele ndayi laru ala	Our departed fathers (ancestors)
Anu abia onworu maya	Come and drink wine
Agbara zi ichi che	All manner of spirits
Anu bia gweru oke kanu	*You all should come and take your share*
Tha otu nwo anu	Today one of your sons
Ge eshilem Nu osodulem	Has proved that he has come of age
Nu owu Obiri nu edere ezi ah	To erect *Obiri* in his homestead
Nu ihi kah	For this reason
Ayi nu orior anu dum	We implore you all (the deities)
Anu ko nkor nu obiri awaah	To always be present in this *Obiri*
Ayi noru nu Obiri awaah no zuike	If we stay in this *Obiri* to rest
Mo obu kpu ele ije	Or to host our guests
He ojoor dakwa shi ayi	Let no harm befall us
Nye bururu he ojoor bia kwu shi ayi	He who visits us with evil
He ojoor kpa ihu	Let evil meet with him
Ayi kwa pula ari oha nu obiriah	If we offer our sacrifices in this *Obiri*
Anu na kweru	Let it be accepted by you
He dum ayi noruru nu obiriah bu onu	Whatever we have cursed in this *Obiri*
Oreeh	Let it be efficacious

He dum ayi gosiri nu obiriah Obiri	What ever we have blessed in this
Oreeh	Let it be efficacious
Nnadi obula am	Kinsmen, is it not so?
Iyaah obu yaah	Yes, it is. [8]

After the prayer, the livestock was slaughtered and its blood allowed to drop on the floor of the main entrance leading into the *Obiri*. The livestock was later cooked with tubers of yam and eaten by all present. In this way the *Obiri* had been consecrated and ready for use. With the performance of this ritual the *Obiri* would cease to be just an ordinary resting hut but a centre for religious rituals. Consequently it was to be looked upon and treated with great awe.

Material Location and Symbolism

There were important items with rich symbolic meanings which could be found in the *Obiri*. First, the sitting arrangement in the *Obiri* was such that the head of the family sat backing the homestead and directly facing *Onu Obiri* (the main entrance leading into the *Obiri*). *Onu Obiri* was symbolic in many respects. It was at the *Onu Obiri* that the head of the family stood to say prayers and pour out libation during rituals. Again, it was believed that it was equally through the *Onu Obiri* that the ancestors and other spirits made their entrance into and took their exit of the *Obiri*. As a result, people were cautioned not to sit as to block the *Onu Obiri* as this might prevent the ancestors and other benevolent spirits from coming into the *Obiri*. More dangerously, it could also spell doom for such a person as he could be struck with untoward event by the spirits in their attempt to gain access into the *Obiri*.

Often hung at one corner of the roof of *Obiri* was the skull of *ehi* (native cow) (in the remote past this was human skull) which was slaughtered at the demise of the head of the family. For instance, Talbot reports that the skulls of all human victims slain for funeral rites were placed as ornaments in the *Obiri*[9]. This, at once, suggested to every visitor that the head of the family was dead and gone to join his ancestors. Sometime, in the distant past, there could also be found hung round the roof of *Obiri* skulls of slain prisoners of war. Talbot further reports the case of the father of one Gabriel Amakiri yellow who was a great warrior and who once went fighting in Omuanwa area. There he took away prisoners whom, he afterwards, gave to his friend Chief Wawuije of Alimini (Isiokpo). The latter, according to Talbot, killed them all and used their skulls to decorate his Obiri[10].

Also hung round the roof of *Obiri* were skulls of wild games that the head of the family had killed in his hunting expeditions. These skulls of animals and humans symbolized the strength and valour of the head of the family who might either be a renowned hunter or a notable warrior. They also conferred prestige and glamour on the family and seen as a hallmark of achievement.

It was also usually on the roof of *Obiri* that families hung the chairs, market baskets and fufu molars of each dead woman of the household together with the barrels which contained the gunpowder used at the funeral ceremonies of the head of the family. This, perhaps, was to serve as a memorial.

Sometimes, in a section of the *Obiri* was carved out an enclosure where the ancestral cult was enshrined. This was the most sacred part of the *Obiri*. The presence of the ancestral cult suggested that though the head of the family was dead and gone to the spirit world; spiritually he was still present in the homestead. For he could still make his intensions known, and his living descendants could still communicate and commune with him through the ancestral cult.

Custodianship, Administration & Taboos Relating to *Obiri*

The custody and the administration of *Obiri* rested on the shoulders of the male founder of the family/lineage. At his demise, the responsibility shifted to the eldest male member of the family/lineage who traced his origin in an unbroken line to the family/lineage founder. He was described as *Nye nosegwu onu Obiri* (the person in-charge of *Obiri*). He was in-charge of all rituals that were carried out in the *Obiri*. He was assisted by his *Nye Mgbaso Igwe* (lieutenant), who was usually the man next in age to the family head. Sometimes too, he was assisted by one of his sons, preferable the eldest. Such favoured son had the privilege of always hanging around when his father had visitors. In addition, through participation in rituals and continued attendance in matters relating to *Obiri* he would become very vast in the traditions of his people. It was his duty and those of other sons of the lineage/family to sweep the *Obiri*, arrange seats and help to entertain visitors. Note that the custody of the *Obiri* did not descend from father to son in immediate succession, but to the eldest surviving son of the family/lineage, who as we have just noted, must trace his ancestry in an unbroken line to the family/lineage founder.

The *Obiri* itself was surrounded by a number of taboos. Amongst these were a taboo forbidden menstruating women and women not properly dressed from going into *Obiri*; a woman who had not reached menopause from sweeping *Obiri*. The reason was that *Obiri* was a sacred place that housed important ritual objects and ancestral emblems. Any contact with a menstruating woman or a woman not fully dressed was believed to pollute and defile such ritual objects. Again, in the event of any argument in the *Obiri*, it was forbidden to strike one's hand on the table. This was regarded not only as an affront to the custodian of the *Obiri*, but also to the ancestors, who, it was believed, were always present in the *Obiri*. Equally, for the same reason, men were forbidden to enter into *Obiri* with caps on their heads. It was a mark of disrespect for the custodian and the ancestors. Also, one was not expected to sit as to block the *Onu Obiri* (the main entrance into the *Obiri*). As we noted earlier, it was believed that this could prevent the ancestors and other benevolent spirits from coming into the *Obiri*. People were not expected to swear falsely in the *Obiri* as every oath taken in the *Obiri* was believed to be very efficacious and binding. Furthermore, people were also forbidden to cry in the *Obiri* as this might evoke the pity of the ancestors who might come to revenge on behalf of the crying person. It was also forbidden for an accused man to sit on the bare floor while others were seated on chairs. This gesture was a way of telling the ancestors that he was being unjustly accused by his opponent. This might anger the ancestors who would quickly intervene on behalf of the aggrieved man.

So far, it is very glaring that *Obiri* played very significant roles in the socio-religious life of the Ikwerre. To flout any of the taboos might not only spell doom and catastrophe for the offender but also for the entire family or lineage group. Again, the various taboos did not only help to instill discipline but ensured social order among the Ikwerre. Also, *Obiri* could be said to have helped in fostering unity and made for easy governance. This was so because the *Nye nosegwu onu Obiri* (the custodian of *Obiri*) was very closely associated with the ancestors and so was highly revered by members of his family/lineage who also owed him tremendous allegiance.

Obiri and Agents of Modern Change

What we have presented so far were Ikwerre beliefs and practices relating to *Obiri* at least on the eve of colonial rule and Christain irruption. However, it is worthy of note that by the last decade of the 19th century, British colonial government began to make in-roads into most Ikwerre towns and villages; so also were Christian missionaries and agents, establishing in their wake Western style education and Christianity. More especially, the construction of the new township of Port Harcourt in 1913 set in motion chains of events that were to accelerate the exposure of Ikwerre land to the twin agents of modernity, namely urbanization and industrialization. The discovery of oil and the subsequent status of Port Harcourt as "oil rich city" attracted the influx of people in search of oil wealth and these gave impetus to a massive dislocation of traditional institutions.

Today, no doubt, the old Port Harcourt township is over populated and the infrastructures stretched beyond their limits. The neighbouring Ikwerre towns have become suburbs for the overcrowded Port Harcourt township. More significantly as S.C. Achinewhu notes in Rivers State, the Ikwerre ethnic nation has made the highest contribution of land to the Federal and state Governments and to individuals for industrial and residential purposes. The oil companies such as Shell, Agip and Elf that operate on Ikwerre land have also taken a chunk of land for oil prospecting, for wells, pipelines, flow stations, roads and office accommodation. This has not only deprived the native of their means of livelihood but has also made land in Ikwerre a piece of expensive hot cake[11]. Consequently, as we shall see in what follows, the Ikwerre attitudes to and use of *Obiri* are fast changing.

Impact of Colonial Rule
Colonial rule has brought tremendous changes on the *Obiri*. Colonialism brought the establishment of Western system of law and order, which must be obeyed. With this, human sacrifices and the display of human parts became very serious offences punishable by law. As a result, human skulls are no longer used in the decoration of *Obiri*.

Impact of Christianity

Perhaps, Christianity more than any other agent of change, has brought significant changes on the location, custodianship, rites, taboos and the general uses of *Obiri*. Very remarkable is the fact that some professing Christians forbid *Obiri* to be built in their homestead, as they argue that *Obiri* is associated with ancestor worship. Even when some are tolerant enough to build *Obiri* it is no longer located in its original place where it was conspicuous and enjoyed prominence; instead it is now situated in an awkward location, preferably at a corner of the compound with the non-observance of all the rituals and taboos relating to it. Thus nowadays *Obiri* is fast loosing its dignity and position in some Ikwerre homesteads.

Equally remarkable is the fact that the administration of *Obiri* has been neglected as more and more of the custodians are becoming members of one Christian denomination or the other and do no longer see the need to attend to the rites associated with *Obiri*. This is corroborated by the fact that in the course of gathering information for this essay most of the *Obiri* we visited had not witnessed any ritual performance in recent time.

Similarly, settlement of disputes and reconciliations between two or more families or lineage members which hitherto was carried out in the *Obiri* and presided over by the *Nye nosegwu onu Obiri* are nowadays carried out in the church. It seems that it is against this background Okechukwu Amadi notes that in Africa today, most of the roles of the traditional priest such as prophecy and settling of disputes are gradually being taken over by the Christian priest who not only acts as a soothsayer but also as a mediator in dispute between individuals and families who might be members of his church.[12] Chima Amadi attributes the preference of the Christian priest and the Christian God to the traditional gods in settling disputes on the ground that the latter is expensive and metes out punishment without delay so that the guilty may not have the opportunity to ask for forgiveness.

Furthermore, many of the taboos associated with *Obiri* are now being flouted with impunity by Christians. For instance, many Ikwerre Christians no longer remove their caps when entering into *Obiri* as doing so is regarded by them as owing double allegiance to God and to the ancestors. Equally, menstruating Christian women enter *Obiri* without the fear of defiling it, so also young Christian women sweep *Obiri*. Indeed, most of the taboos relating to *Obiri* which do not conform to Christian doctrines are treated with disregard by Christians. It is against this background that A.C. Amadi strongly notes that as educated people, Ikwerre Christians have virtually ceased to prostrate before the *Owhor* holder and do not even remove their caps in his presence. This, he concludes, is undermining the authority of the *Owhor* holder and traditional Ikwerre religion generally[14].

Perhaps, the most remarkable change which Christianity has brought on the *Obiri* bothers on its usage. It is worthy of note that many Christian denominations, especially those of the Pentecostal family, are gradually taking over *Obiri* as a place of worship. This is particularly alarming of the Port Harcourt area where due to scarcity of accommodation and its rising cost, it has now become a common sight every evening and on Sundays to see various Christian denominations worship in the *Obiri*, clapping hands and singing praises. An example here is the Young Servants of God Outreach that worships at *Obiri* Chindah of Oroabali.

While some Ikwerre Christians see this development as a postive change, in the assessment of some Ikwerre traditionalists, this has led to the desecration of *Obiri*. They are thus inclined to reason that the presence of Christian sects is driving away the ancestors. It is on this note that Innocent Amadi argues that Ikwerre traditional institutions have undergone tremendous changes and are fast losing their positions in the socio-political and religious lives of the people. He is of the opinion that the changes which Christianity brought have distorted Ikwerre religious heritage to the point that most of the *Obiri* have lost their sacredness. As a result, they can now be best described as mere family reception halls, predominantly serving social functions[15]. In a similar vein, Dopamu and Awolalu, writing on the impact of Christianity and Islam on West African traditional religion generally observe that the incursion of Christianity and Islam have acted as a social force which has played down the significance of traditional religion. As a result, certain customs have died a natural or forced death, while many traditional practices have either crumbled or disappeared[16].

Indeed, as we noted earlier, many Ikwerre sons and daughters have become professing Christians. As a result, they no longer participate in most of the rites connected with *Obiri*. While some traditionalists sit in *Obiri* and participate in the rituals, their Christian kinsmen often describe them as ancestor worshippers and call them all sorts of names. This situation, thus is fast eroding family/lineage solidarity and unity as people no longer speak with one voice and act in unison on matters relating to *Obiri*.

Impact of Urbanization and Industrialization

Like Christianity, urbanization and industrialization, have also brought far reaching changes on the *Obiri*. Urbanization has made acquisition of land for the erection of *Obiri* very difficult. Land pressure, especially on the Ikwerre in the Diobu area of Port Harcourt, has made it practically impossible for the people to earmark a portion of land for the purpose of erecting *Obiri*. This is because land has become a very important income earner which must be judiciously utilized for monetary gains. Consequently, in most Ikwerre urban centres, available pieces of land are sold out to land developers or used for community or government projects. The need for land to be used for *Obiri* is, therefore, relegated to the background. So, urbanization has brought pressure on land which has forced many people to resort to using their sitting–rooms as *Obiri*. The modern architectural designs which create enough space in the sitting- room for virtually every aspect of life has given more impetus to this.

Equally remarkable is the positive change which technology is bringing to bear on the construction of *Obiri*. Today, *Obiri* is constructed with "block and zinc", and indeed, there are many magnificent *Obiri* that are masterpieces of modern architectural designs.

Western education has also brought tremendous influence on the changes going on in the *Obiri*. It has detached people from their traditional environment and exposed them to a Western orientated life pattern. Those schooled in Western education feel highly sophisticated and would not want to have much to do with *Obiri* and its associated rituals and taboos. More so, when it is the turn of such people to assume the position of *Nye nosegwu onu Obiri*, they often decline to do so. When in extreme cases they accept to assume the position they shirk most of the responsibilities and neglect most of the rituals. An informant described such a custodian as a figure head whose duty is only to go by the title *Nye nosegwu onu Obiri* without carrying out the religious functions attached to the position.[17]

It is also note worthy that the demands of civil service jobs and the search for "golden fleece" have forced many people away from home. Nowadays, the person considered most appropriate by reason of his age and ancestry for the office of *Nye nosegwu Onu Obiri* may be one of the many who reside and work in one of the cities outside Ikwerre land, and who come home only at intervals. Such persons, sometimes, may be willing to be installed as *Nye nosegwu Onu Obiri* but their incumbency gives rise to problems stemming from their long absence, and in some cases, from their reluctance to perform non-Christian religious duties. A common response to such problems has been the creation of the post of a caretaker, whose principal duties are to perform rituals addressed to the family or lineage ancestors and to look after their shrines in the absence of the substantive office holder. This practice, however, has its own pitfalls, as in some cases, the care-taker may not be willing to relinquish power on the return of the *bona fide Nye nosegwu onu Obiri*; a situation which has sometimes given rise to chieftaincy squabbles.

It is against this background that Dopamu and Awolalu bemoaned the fate of West African traditional religion generally. According to them, in many localities genuine votaries are dying out. Where priesthood is hereditary, those who are to become priests or priestesses are sometimes not available because they have either gone to school or learnt a new trade. Old men are allowed to take charge of the cults. This, according to Awolalu and Dopamu, constitutes a big set back for the traditional religion. Similarly, they observe that the indigenous religion is becoming increasingly outmoded, especially among the educated people. They further note that many people who have been exposed to foreign cultures think that the indigenous religion is 'primitive' and should not be encouraged, contending that the religion is full of barbaric acts and practices which should not have been allowed to remain on the face of the earth.[18]

It should be emphasized here the remarkable impact of Western style education and urbanization in undermining the indigenous religious use of *Obiri*. Today *Obiri* is increasingly being used for social and secular purposes. It is now common place to see people holding parties, social and business meetings in *Obiri*. Most worrisome to the traditionalists is the fact that some *Obiri* nowadays have been converted into schools by private school owners. Thus, in the course of this research, we noticed that the *Obiri* of Wobo family of Oroabali community has been taken over by Steve Ture Educational Centre. Similarly, Saint Mike's Nursery and Primary School now conducts business in the *Obiri* of Owhor family of Oroabali community. The implication of all this, as we have earlier noted, is that *Obiri* is fast loosing its awe and sacredness as a centre of religious rituals.

Opinions, however, differ on how the Ikwerre themselves see this on-going change. Most Ikwerre Christians see it as a positive development. In their own words: "It is the triumph of Christendom over paganism"[19]. Similarly, the educated Ikwerre are also of the view that the on-going change is an obvious sign of the overall impact of Western civilization on the Ikwerre and their socio-cultural and religious institutions. To them, the change is welcome insofar as it helps to transform society[20]. On the other hand, the core traditionalists see nothing good in this change which to them is rapidly eroding Ikwerre cultural heritage. Moreso, they now attribute low fertility, unproductive harvest and crop failure to the neglect and desecration of *Obiri* by non traditionalists.

Conclusion

Our examination of the socio-religious functions of *Obiri* in the life of the Ikwerre has shown that *Obiri* was an indispensable institution in Ikwerre traditional society. Beginning from birth, through adolescence to adulthood and even at death, *Obiri* was the centre of an array of socio-religious activities which provided meaning and under girded the life of individuals, families and even the village group. In spite of its socio-religious functions, it also helped in the governance of the people as the eldest male who was usually in charge of *Obiri* was highly respected by members of the family/lineage because of his perceived close association with the ancestors and other patron deities.

However, with the advent of Christianity and other agents of modern change remarkable transformation and change were witnessed not only on the beliefs and practices relating to *Obiri* but also on its physical structure. In the light of the above, scenario, the pertinent question is: what is the future of *Obiri* in the life of the Ikwerre? To answer this question we have to note that the changes which *Obiri* has witnessed, by and large, are circumstantially positive. The *Obiri* institution will not go into extinction rather it will continue to exert a good measure of attraction taking into cognizance the new and emerging social order.

Notes and References

1. The Ikwerre live on the north-eastern fringes of the Niger Delta of Nigeria.
2. P.A. Talbot *Tribes of the Niger Delta* (London: Frank Cass, 1967) p. 273.
3. Oral interview with chief Aleruchi Ogoloma, 78 yrs old, farmer, Oroworukwo town, 15/12/2003
4. Oral interview with Chief Johnson Odum, 70 yrs old, palm wine tapper, Rumuji town, 20/12/2003
5. Oral interview with Elder Bekwelem Chinda, 75 yrs old, farmer, Oroabali town, 10/11/1003
6. Talbot, p. 273
7. This ritual text was offered by Elder Wosumali Worlu, 75 yrs old, farmer, Aluu town, 15/10/2002
8. This ritual text was offered by Elder Worlu.
9. Talbot, p. 250
10. Talbot, p. 250
11. S.C. Achineewhu (ed.), *The Case of Ikwerre Ethnic Nationality* (Port Harcourt: Link Advertising, 1994), p. 27
12. Okechukwu Amadi "Ikwerre Traditional Religion" Unpublished Long Essay. Dept. of Religious Studies, Rivers State College of Education, Port Harcourt, 1990. p.5
13. Chima Amadi "The Roles of Priests in Ikwerre Traditional Society" Unpublished Long Essay. Dept.

of Religious Studies, Rivers State College of Education, Port Harcourt, 1990. p. 7

14. Aman Amadi "Religion and Change in Ikwerre" Unpublished Long Essay. Dept. of Religious Studies, Rivers State College of Education, Port Harcourt, 1990. p. 21.

15. Oral interview with Chief Ibejirika Amadi, 71 yr old, family head, Rumuolumeni town, 10/10/2003.

16. J.O. Awolalu and P.A. Dopamu *West African Traditional Religion* (Ibadan: Onibonoje Press, 1978) p. 280

17. Oral interview with Elder Alikwu Amadi, 62 yrs old, Commnuity leader and traditionalist, Rumuolumeni town, 10/10/2003

18. Awolalu and Dopamu, pp. 282 and 279

19. This is the view of the following informants:
    (a) Joyce Amadi, Ibaa town, 20/10/2003
    (b) Amaehule Njoku, Ibaa town, 20/10/2003
    (c) James Amadi, Aluu town, 14/10/2003
    (d) Opurum Nyeche, Ogbogoro town, 30/10/2003

20. This is the view of the following informants. They are mainly undergraduate students drawn from the University of Port Harcourt.
    (a)   Agness, Chindah, 11/11/202
    (b)   Jacob Amadi, 11/11/2003
    (c)   Amadi Chindah, 12/11/2003

(d)   Iheayi Okpobiri, 12/11/2003

21. This is the view of the following informants:
    (a)   Elder Elikwu Amadi, 78 yr old, Egbeda town, 20/10/2002
    (b)   Chief Chimadi Wosa, 75 yr old, Egbeds town, 20/10/2002
    (c)   Chief James Ogbu, 80 yr old, Ubimini town, 20/10/2003.

5. The Use of *Dunamis* in Mark

J. Enuwosa
Dept. of Religious Studies, Delta State University, Abraka.
Email – jenuwosa@juno.com

Introduction
One of the terms, which Mark frequently used, is *dunamis*. Mark used *dunamis* to translate the Hebrew act of power. The term has a notable development from "ability, capacity to the concept of might and power."[1] In Mark, much theological importance is attached to it. In the Hellenistic world, *dunamis* is the causal efficiency that moves the world. To the Greeks, "the life of the cosmos was conceived dynamically. The cosmic principle is filled with effective force and is thus a dynamic magnitude, which fashions all things"[2]. To some scholars, this Greek conception of power did influence Mark.[3] The study is also intended to show the significance of *dunamis*.

Power is the force with which we control a thing. This is a general definition of power. In the religious sense, power is an apparent phenomenon of the inner consciousness illuminated by the divine through faith or ritual. This is quite different from mechanical and scientific use of power. In electrical and mechanical sciences, it is seen as energy, potency, motion, force. It is regarded in pure sciences as the rate of work, which the agent can perform in a given time, the force exerted on a job done in a given period of time. It can also be defined in science as the force applied to overcome resistance. The notion of force, rate or exertion that produces some effects are also found in the religious usage. Power causes change when it reaches the object on which it is acting upon. It is invariably the cause of every change. The vital question here is how is the complex concept of religio-psychological power expressed on the physical plane? Fechner's theory provides the answer.[4]

According to Fechner, "this increase of sensation is the logarithm of the stimulus. In every energy increase in the square of velocity in the physical world, there is a correspondence to the stimulus increase by a similar law in the psychic world."[5] This is the formula to which the facts of our sensitive consciousness curiously happen to conform. This operates in organic and inorganic world. It is more than a natural law. It is a fundamental metaphysical law governing the relations of the physical to the psychical and conversely the psychical to the physical. This is called "psycho-physical parallelism."[6] Something, therefore, holds the relation of potential-power energy between the physical and the spiritual. It is reasonable to say that the actual nature of this power - act in the psychic world are sometime experienced in our objective world. This is the intended usage of power in

Mark's gospel. He employed the term with a religious undertone. This *dunamis* for Mark is the power with which Jesus was constituted and performed his miracle through the agency of the Holy Spirit.

Markan Application of *Dunamis*

But according to W. Grundmann, the meaning of *dunamis* in the New Testament is determined by the Biblical usage.[7] The difference between the Greek and Markan conception of power is obvious. The great deeds of the Greek deity are identified with impersonal power, which must be controlled, by ritual actions and incantations. This is the factor of magic, cultic ceremony and ritual. In Mark's gospel, one is dealing with the personal God who is the Lord of history with whom one may enter into relationship. One must seek him to influence his will by obedience, faith and prayer. The associated view of power is, therefore, very different. Thus, *dunamis* is suitable to denote the miracles of Jesus Christ. When used in the context of Mark, it retains its capacity to designate the extraordinary, the miraculous. This emancipates the concept of miracle emancipated from the connotations clinging to it from its profane secular environs.

According to C. David, *dunamis* is the "significant manifestations of God's power." This to him is the power of God, which dwelt in Jesus.[8] For R. E. Brown *dunamis* is the power of God to salvation manifested in Jesus.⁹ Moule's and Brown's meaning are attempt to distinguish the gospel miracles from those of the Greek gods. By implication, the miracle in Greek mythology does not reveal the power of God. In order to explain *dunamis*, one may need to indicate in Marcan context the relationship between power, the act of power and the person of Jesus. Moreover, the background to Mark's use of the terms has to be explained.

The term in Mark has a closer affinity with the Old Testament. In the Old Testament, Israel's experience in the Exodus and the Sea of Reed led to the conception of the mighty act of God, the power of Yahweh (Exod. 12:14; Deut. 3:24). This faith came to include a further use of the power of Yahweh in history (Neh 1:10; Isa. 10:33). God's power shapes and fashion's history according to his will and purpose. Mark saw a close connection between the power of Christ and the power of God. To him, the power of Christ is the power of God.

The might and power of the Messiah is described in the Old Testament (Isa. 9:5; 11:12; Micah 5:5).¹⁰ The picture of the Messiah in these passages is of a king who in a victorious power conquers his foes. The Messiah is the one believed to be endowed with this strength and power of Yahweh. Jesus, therefore, as the Christ is the unique bearer of the power of God according to Mark. By personal fellowship, he shares in this divine power. In this way, the power of God which is active in history rests in Jesus as the Christ.

In another dimension, Mark used *dunamis* as the eschatological exercise of God's power in Jesus to overthrow demonic powers. In Christ, the power of God which shapes and fashions history is active. This is the decisive meaning of the term in Mark. Thus, the predominant trait is not force or power, but the will which this power executes and serves. The term, therefore, comes to mean the creative power of God in Christ to provide physical salvation. Understood in this sense, it is the active power of God at work in Jesus. It is the dynamic activity of the divine in a saving action. David believes that *dunamis* is fundamentally the power of the living God, or a "mighty work" which manifests his power.[11] V. Taylor was correct when he said *dunamis* is "the divine healing power which dwells in Jesus (Mk. 5:30; Lk 5:17) and proceeds from him (Lk 6:19)."[12]

Mark used *dunamis* as a special word to designate the miracles of Jesus for certain reasons. J. Francis has given two major reasons why Mark used power for miracles. Mark, according to Moule, has used power and avoided the normal words for miracles (marvel, sign, portent) because these words were used to describe the deeds of Greek gods. Mark, therefore, intended to differentiate the miracles of Jesus from pagan miracles.[13] According to H. Rengstorf, irrational portents were attributed to Zeus.

They were spectacular works of wonders, marvel and magic.[14] Francis' second reason is that Mark avoided the words, 'sign' and 'portents' because they were used by false prophets and false messiahs to deceive people.[15]

Mark's use of power for the miracles of Jesus may not in itself distinguish the miracles of Jesus from those of the Greek gods.[16] This is because there was no specific word reserved for the miracles of Jesus in the early Church. Each person was describing the miracles as best as he could in the early Church. Hence different words were used in the gospels for the miracles.

Justin Martyr used power to show the wonders done by Hebrew prophets and false prophets.[17] Celsus accused Jesus of going to Egypt to acquire power on the basis of which he proclaimed himself a god.[18] Origen described the *dunamis* of Jesus as significant power.[19] Thus *dunamis* was not a monopoly of Mark. It was used by others to describe miracles in general in the early Church and in the ordinary society of the first two centuries.

The Relationship between *Dunamis* & *Thaumazo* in Mark

There is a collection between *dunamis* and *thaumazo*. *Thaumazo* means marvel. It has its root in *thea*, vision, or reflection. G. Bertram thinks that the adjective was used at the time of Hesiod. But at the time of Homer, it has changed into a verbal adjective, *thaumastos*.[20] C.F.D.

Moule believes that *thaumazo* was rarely used in the first century A.D. Hence the word has almost become extinct in the New Testament.[21] The word appears in Greek Old Testament (LXX). It occurs in Proverbs 6:30. Here in this passage, it is used as a rhetorical formula. In Job 42:11, *ethaumasan* reminds us of the wonderful direction of God which Job had experienced. "He raised him out of his lowliness and lifts up his head and many are astonished at him."

The substitute, *thauma,* is also used three times in Job (17:8, 18:20; 21:5). It expresses the horror which grips those who must watch the judgment of God. The phrase, *plegai thaumastai,* in Deuteronomy. 28:59 and the verb in Lev. 26:32 have this sense. *Thaumasta erga* in Exodus 34:10 has the meaning of Yahweh's wonderful direction of his people. The use of *thaumazo* in the Old Testament bears the mark of wonder and astonishment in wisdom literature (Prov 6:30; Job 42:11; 18:8; 18:20; Deut 28:59; Ex 34:10; Lev 26:32). In the New Testament, the term takes on a more basic theological precision. In general, Mark's usage often occurs at the end of his miracle stories. It is primarily used to show the effect of the miracles of Jesus on the spectators. At the end of the healing of the Gerasene demoniac, Mark says *pantes ethaumazon* (all were astonished, Mark 5: 20).

The expression of man's attitude to the divine from the standpoint of religious psychology underlines Mark's use of *thaumazo*. This may take various forms. It is either awesome astonishment at the divine, or a critical surprises which resists, or which did not understand the ministry of Jesus. Sometimes it takes the form of an honest and acceptable admiration. These are variously expressed in Mark 2:12; 4:41; 5:20; 6:6, 51; 7:37; 12:11: 17; 15:5, 55: 16:8). In all cases, it is used by Mark to emphasize the self-evident nature of a thing not understood by man in his attitude to the divine. It is an outward expression of the innermost feeling at what has happened. For this reason, G. Bertran said: "our word, *thaumazo* is an expression of faith in the wonderful ways of God which in the first instance man cannot understand."[22] We would, therefore, seem to agree with his conclusion that:

> *If there is any expression of the divine mystery which awakens dread, those who know astonishment are still in the forecourt. The human attitude of astonishment at the numinous is not yet faith. At most it is only a preliminary stage of faith, or in psychological terms, the impulse which may awaken faith but which may also give rise to doubt.*[23]

Matthew and Luke have this meaning of astonishment as well (Mt 8:34; 9:33; 12:23; Lk 8:39; 11:4). Luke prefers to use *paradozon* (surprising). *Thaumazo* is used in much the same way in the teaching of Jesus as in the miracle stories by Mark. The bearers are surprised at his eloquence which they hardly expect from a man of his origin. *Thaumazo* here is made clearer by Luke's use of *logoi tes karitos* (words of grace, 4:22). By this, he refers to the outward charm of the words of Jesus and its inward content as a proclamation of grace. The rejection of Jesus at Nazareth and the debate about taxes embody this usage (Mk 6:2-3; 12:17; Mt 22:22; Lk 20:26). In Mark 6:6, Jesus himself showed an astonishment at the unbelief in Nazareth. In Matthew and Luke, the faith of the Capernaum centurion provoked his astonishment (Mt. 8:10; Lk 7:9). Doubt and fear are combined with *thaumazo* at the astonishment of Pilate in Mark 15:44 and the story of the empty tomb (Mk 15:44; 16:8). In John's gospel, *thaumazo* is a term for the impact made by the works of Jesus (Jn 5:20; 7:21).

According to Moule, the term is not frequently used because the disciples did not regard Jesus' miracles as great deeds of wonder. Rather they saw the power of God in the works of Jesus. [24] It was avoided because it was commonly used in mystery religions of the period. Moreover, Greek philosophical element entered the rich Old Testament meaning of *thaumazo*. The supernatural element and the revelation of God's mighty power in miracle were influenced by Hellenistic culture. Miracle in Judaism came to be seen from the point of view of Greek idea. In Hellenistic world, miracle is regarded as marvelous or wonderful deeds of the gods. When some Jews embraced Hellenism, they accepted the Greek idea of the laws of nature. They were not able to reconcile the laws of nature in a universe where things work by cause and effect with the belief on the power of Yahweh. Yahweh is the God who delivered Israel from Egypt with mighty power. Yahweh in Israel acts in human history from heaven. This use of power in Mark is closely related to the use of sign in John's gospel.

Dunamis in Mark and *Semeion* in John

The word for miracle in the gospel of John is sign. *Semeion* (sign, mark, pointer) is a term seldomly used in Mark for the miracles of Jesus. *Semeion* only surfaced seven times in Mark, but in all cases it was not used as another word for miracle by Mark (Mk 7:24; 8:11; 12; 13:4, 22, 25). The opponents of Jesus regarded his miracles as signs. Hence, they demanded for signs to prove that the power and authority by which Jesus performed miracles came from God. In Mark 8:11 sign was demanded from Jesus. Mark described the miracles of Jesus as graet deeds of power. The demand for sign is related to the miracles of Jesus in which his authority and power are revealed. In this demand, Jesus was asked to show that his power and authority by which he worked miracles were from God.[25] They wanted to know if Jesus has really come from God. Mark probably avoided the term 'sign,' because the idea conveys acts of false Satanic works.

In Mark 13:4, sign is used in an apocalyptic sense. The sign in the sun, moon and stars in Mark 13:23 are underlined by the apocalyptic passages of Isaiah 13:10 and 24:4. It describes eschatological events which indicate that the last time is dawning. Using the words of K.H. Rengstorf, if signs are miraculous it is simply because one may see from them that the order of creation is beginning to disintegrate.[26]

John's distinctive use of *semeion* takes the place of Markan *dunamis* (Jn 5:30, 36; 7:3, 21; 2:1-10). It is an exclusive term for miracle in John. Sign is a significant act which conveys a meaning that is deeper than the actual event. The fourth evangelist, therefore, has used sign for his own view of the power in Jesus. *Semeion* in John is the acts of the Messiah done out of the fullness of messianic power. In this way, the signs in John are acts which point to the power of God in Jesus. There are some differences in the use of *dunamis* in Mark and *semeion* in John. Mark believed that the gospel miracles were works done by the power of God in Jesus. John used sign to show that the miracles point to the power of God inside Jesus. It is the means by which God is revealed in His work of judgment and salvation.

The power of Jesus in Mark is capable of coming out of his inner self or his divine being to accomplish the acts of miracles. But the power of Jesus, which works miracles in the gospel of John, remains inside him. Thus, while Mark insisted that the miracles were great manifestation of the actual power of God, John thought that the miracles point to God's power. Hence R.C. Trench concluded that "*Semeion* is a kind of finger-post of God indicative of the grace and power of the doer, or of his immediate connection with a higher spiritual world"[27] Mark used sign to mean a spectacular wonder. For Mark sign is an eschatological event, which will show that the end of time is near (Mk. 13:24f).

Signs for John are also eschatological events. To those who believed, the miracles of Jesus are signs which feed their faith (Jn 5:30, 36; 7:3, 21). To those who did not believe, signs may be multiplied indefinitely without producing any faith (Jn 3:18, 36; Mk 4:11). John has also employed sign in a symbolic way. It is the means by which he communicates the challenge of the person and work of Jesus. The signs are symbolic stories because they bring out the theological meaning of the person of Jesus. Leon Morris thus argued that "John has used sign to explain the implicit Christology in the synoptic miracles. He clarified the synoptic Christology and stamped it on the miracle materials in a manner that the reader cannot escape it. To understand the miracles as signs is to apprehend Christ by faith (Jn 20: 30-31)."[28]

The plagues in Egypt are supreme miracles. They pointed to the saving power of God (Exod. 5:14). This physical deliverance of the Exodus constitutes the primary focus of the Old Testament. John focused his attention on the spiritual meaning of Jesus' miracles. This does not mean that the material action of the miracles can be dispensed with. Rather while less emphasis is placed on the material results of miracles, John puts great emphasis on their spiritual values.[29] For example, the healing of the noble man's son is the manifestation of Christ's glory (Jn 4: 43-52). The healing of the paralytic man at the pool of Bethzatha reveals that Jesus is the Messiah (Jn 5: 1-9). This is the picture of the new age of God that the lame shall leap like a hart (Isa. 35:6).[30]

The discourse that follows those two miracles points out that the life which Jesus gives is a spiritual life (Jn 5"21,-24). This meaning is clearly shown in the raising of Lazarus (Jn11: 1-44). The restoration of physical life to Lazarus is, therefore, important only as a sign of eternal life.[31] John, however, is still in harmony with the tradition of Mark that miracles are the manifestation of the power of God in Jesus. John believed that Jesus was acting with the power of the Father. He too saw them as the natural expressions of divine sympathy for suffering humanity. This prompted C.K. Barret to say that "the miracles in John are set in a context of human need." This ranges from the deficiency of wine at a wedding feast to the death of Lazarus and the death of Jesus for the sin of the world.[32]

The miracles as signs point beyond themselves to the revelation of the saving power of God in his Son as the plagues in Egypt pointed to the saving power of Yahweh (Exod. 5-15). John for this reason designated the miracles of Jesus as signs and described them as his works. These works John also regarded as the works of God himself (Jn 5: 36; 9:3; 10:32, 37; 14-10). While Jesus accomplished the work of the Father as an obedient Son (Jn 4:34), the Father manifested his miraculous power in him (Jn 14:34), the works therefore manifested both the character and the power of God which indicates that he is active in Jesus in a unique way.

Dunamis and *semeion* for the evangelists have profound implications for the kingdom of God. The terms are used to express their eschatological belief. While Mark used power (*dunamis*) for his consistent eschatology, John employed sign for his realized eschatology. For Mark, the manifestation of the power (*dunamis*) of God in Jesus is the preparation of the followers of Christ for the Kingdom of God. The disciples have to be loosed from the power of sins and infirmities. Though the kingdom of God is coming entirely in the future at the end of time, the people must be prepared to enter the kingdom. Meanwhile, we have only the church, which is radically different from the kingdom where the people of the household of God would be prepared for the coming of Christ.

The signs for John explain the work and presence of the kingdom. In John's realized eschatology, Christ occupies the place of God as both subject and object in the divine-human relationship. The relation of Jesus to the father is the archetype, the paradigm. God is known in Christ because Jesus himself is the true God. He occupies the place of God with all his prerogative rights. So, the age to come has come in Christ. Therefore, the kingdom and the eternal life of God is here and now. Those who believe the historic Jesus have attained eternal life and entered the kingdom of God, which is the real beatific vision of God (1:14). The believer already enjoys eternal life. He is already living in a state, which excludes the possibility of ceasing to be.

The Significance of *Dunamis* in Mark: The Binding Saying

The significance of Mark's choice of *dunamis* for miracle is explained in the binding saying (Mk 3: 22-26). The saying is connected with the Beelzebul accusation in Mark (Mk. 3: 22-26, 27-30; Mt. 12: 29, 31; Lk. 11: 12; 12: 10). In this parable, Jesus interpreted his mission on earth in the gospel of Mark. The use of power (*dunamis*) in

Mark puts the whole narratives on a structural frame of conflict and struggle. The story of the binding of the strong man shows that Jesus was not performing his work of healing and exorcism by the power of Satan. He has come to bind the strong man with the active power of God and the Holy Spirit in him (Mk. 3: 29). The Scribes from Jerusalem levelled two charges against Jesus. The first one is that he had Beelzebul (3: 22), that is he was possessed by demon, evil spirit. His second charge is that he cast out demons by the power of the prince of demons, Satan. Matthew and Luke combined the two charges together, thereby identifying Beelzebul with Satan.

There can be no doubt that Jesus accepted the contemporary belief in the reality of Satan as the lord of the evil powers (Mk. 3: 22).[33] Both the spelling of the name and the derivation of Beelzebul are uncertain. Matthew and Luke have Beelzebul in all cases.[34] It means "Lord of dung." In this usage, it is "Lord of flies." According to B. H. Branscomb, the saying is a product of the apostolic age.[35] V. Taylor thinks that it belongs to an early tradition.[36] This parable may be the saying of Jesus because it reflects the normal accusation levied against most exorcists of every age. Hence R. Bultmann maintained that in the binding saying, the characteristic of the preaching of Jesus is found."[37]

The saying on binding gives the conception of the kingdom of God in Mark a present eschatological setting. Jesus saw his mission as an invasion of the Satanic kingdom by plundering the evil power of his goods. The strong man is a symbolic term for Satan. Jesus is the stronger one. The goods are the sick, the possessed ones enslaved by Satan and sin. This is the interpretation of many commentators.[38] The binding of the evil power as eschatological conception can be traced to Isa. 24: 22; 49: 24. A.E.J. Rawlinson and B. H. Branscomb argued that the one who binds may be God.[39] But it is better to think that Jesus himself is the one binding Satan since he is the power of the kingdom. The problem is not easily solved because if Satan has been bound why is man still suffering?[40]

If Satan has been bound, his wicked activities would have been completely eliminated in our world. Perhaps Jesus was not able to bind him because the evidence of the binding of Satan is not just there in human experience. Since the evil activities of Satan occur in human history, the binding as well should be reflected within the history of human experience. Even Satan is very much shown as active in the subsequent events of Jesus' life. It is, therefore, more plausible to think of the binding as did R. H. Hiers. According to Hiers, the binding is the assumption based on the preliminary victory of God over Satan in the ministry of Jesus.[41]

This world for Mark has drifted away from its original perfect state because there was no sickness in God's initial creation. This opinion is expressed in the entire Scriptures. The world is no longer God's world, but the world of Satanic kingdom. "This evil empire," said J. Kallas, "is to be shattered and God's rule restored. Thus, redemption and creation are intimately linked"[42] in healing and exorcisms. This requires the might of the stronger one to enter the strong man's house to plunder his goods (3: 27). The gospel of Mark is, thus, cast in the form of an eschatological struggle in history. Mark speaks the language of a spiritual warfare (plundering, tormenting, binding). For Mark, therefore, events in the world are by no means ambiguous.

The interpretation of this parable shows that Jesus' miracles were signs of the coming of the kingdom. In the attempt to destroy the deep-seated dominion of Satan, God sent Jesus on an earthly mission to save humanity. Jesus the stronger man assaulted and overcome Satan. This action is the binding of the strong man. For Luke, it is striping Satan of his armour (Mt 1: 2: 22; Lk 11: 11-26). This action released the saving power of God into the world of men. The kingdom of Satan is assaulted in order to transform men into the kingdom of God. Wherever the power of the kingdom is present, the rule of Satan is overcome. Through sickness and affliction, Satan breaks men's trust in God by snatching away their faith (Mk 4: 14). But by healing and exorcisms, Satan is being defeated.

Though Satan is bound and defeated, its activities of sickness, diseases and possession are still felt in the physical world. This is because its final defeat has not yet been made. It will be realized on the second coming of Jesus when the Lord of history will begin the eschatological judgment. This constitutes "the now" and "the not yet" aspects of the kingdom of God in the Messianic age of salvation. Hence Satan is still active.[43]

In the interim, Satan would continue to operate in sickness and diseases. But the Christian would overcome all if he stands in faithful trust of his Lord who has put Satan into flight. R. H. Hiers thus remarked that, "the demons were still far from being finally defeated. But because Jesus had given his followers powers and authority over the unclean spirits, they would prevail."[44] Hence the whole Marcan narratives appear to have been built on a structural frame of conflict and struggle. Though Mark has no intention of proposing a dualistic theology, he has used the medium to combat such belief in order to underline the Christological character of Jesus' person.

Conclusion

Thus, the notion of the power of the kingdom of God is fundamentally important in Mark's use of *dunamis*. The destruction of the kingdom of Satan is a basic eschatological idea in the teaching of Jesus in Mark. The struggle in this conflict situation is between God and Satan. Since the main opponent of God's kingdom is spiritual, the victory of the kingdom of God must first of all be a spiritual victory. The theology, therefore, is that man must first of all be delivered from the spiritual powers which are beyond his ability to control. The coming of God's kingdom and its final establishment on earth means the destruction of the very principle of evil in its spiritual domain. The healing power is related to the kingdom because they are eschatological conquest of Satan by God and his Messiah. The kingdom of God has, therefore, invaded the realm of Satan and has won a preliminary victory. This victory means that members of God's kingdom are now fighting a winning battle while Satan and his hosts are fighting a losing battle.

The study, therefore, reveals the meaning of the basic terms used for miracles in Mark. The meanings are deduced principally from the analysis of word. Critical interpretation uses word analysis to discern the truth of biblical passage. The main aim for Mark was to use the term to explain the relationship of the father to the son. While the son submits himself to the father in obedience, the father in turn manifests his power in his son.

Notes and References

1. W. Grundmann, *"Dunamis," Theological Dictionary of the New Testament.* Vol.II, (Grand Rapids, 1969), 287.
2. Ibid, 286
3. L. Edelstein, *Asclepius, A Collection and Interpretation of the Testimonies,* (Baltimore: Johns Hopkins University Press, 1965) 140
4. A. Fesher, "Psycho-Religious Concept of Power," in *Contemporary Studies of Psychic Behaviour,* Vol. 2, Ed. J. Unwane, (Lagos: New World Communication, 1998), 37.
5. Ibid.
6. Ibid.
7. Grundmann, *Op. Cit.*292
8. C. David, *Words and Synonyms in the New Testament,* (Chicago: Chicago University Press, 1997), 26.
9. R. E. Brown and D. M. Stanley, "Mark," *Jerome Biblical Commentary,* (London, 1993), 287.
10. Isaiah Calls Him a Mighty Hero. Micah says He is a Shepherd in Strength (Micah 5:57).
11. David, *Op. Cit.* 29.
12. V. Taylor, *The Gospel According to St. Mark,* (London: Macmillan, 1963), 298.
13. J. Francis (ed.) *The Terminologies of Synoptic Gospels,* (London: Mowbray, 1966), 57.
14. Ibid.

15. Ibid.
16. H. Remus, "Does Terminology Distinguish Early Christian From pagan miracles," *Journal of Biblical Literature,* Vol. 101, No 4, (Philadelphia, Dec. 1982), 545.
17. Ibid. 550
18. Ibid.
19. Ibid.
20. G. Bertram, "*Thaumazo,*" *Theological Dictionary of the New Testament,* Vol. III, (Grand Rapids, 1969), 31.
21. C. F. D. Moule (ed.) "The Vocabulary of Miracle," in *Miracle,* (London: Mowbray, 1966), 259.
22. Bertram, Op. Cit.
23. Ibid.
24. Moule (ed.), Op. Cit.
25. K. H. Rengstorf, "*Semeion,*" *Theological Dictionary of the New Testament,* Vol. III, (Michigan, 1983), 235.
26. Ibid
27. R. C. Trench, *The Synonyms of New the Testament,* (London: Grand Rapids, 1963), 339.
28. L. Moris, *Studies in the Four Gospels,* (Melbourne: Pater-noster Press, 1969), 51.
29. C. K. Barret, *The Gospel According to St John,* (London: SPCK, 1978), 74.
30. Ibid.
31. V. Taylor, *The Gospel According to St. Mark.* 3rd Edition, (London: Macmillan, 1958), 239.

32. B. P. Westcott and J. F. A. Hort, *The New Testament in the Original Greek, Introduction and Appendix*, (Cambridge: Cambridge University Press, 1881), 159. The form Beelzebul is found in vg. sy^s pe.
33. B. H. Branscomb, *The Gospel of St. Mark*, (New York: Harper and Row, 1963), 132.
34. V. Taylor, *Op. cit.* 240.
35. R. Bultmann, *History of the Synoptic Tradition*, (New York: Harper and Row, 1963), 132.
36. H. B. Swete, *The Gospel According to St. Mark*, (London: Macmillan, 1953), 67. V. Taylor, *Op. cit.* 241. H. Turner, "Marcan Usage: Notes, Critical Exegetical, on the Second Gospel," *Journal of Theological Studies*, Vol. 26, No. 5, (Oxford, 1925), 23. T.W. Manson, *The Saying of Jesus,* 3rd Edition, (London: CUP, 1949), 86.
37. A. E. J. Rawlinson, *The Gospel According to St. Mark*, (London: Methuen, 1952), 44. B. H. Branscomb, *Op. cit.* 71.
38. L. S. Hay, "The Son of God Christology in Mark," *Journal of Biblical Review*, Vol. 32, No. 3, (London: Mowbray, Jan. 1964), 108.
39. R. H. Hiers, "Satan, Demons and the Kingdom of God," *Scottish Journal of Theology*, Vol. 27, No. 1, (Cambridge, Feb. 1974), 45. Cf. G. R. Gardener, "The Gospel Miracles and Contemporary Healers," *The Journal of Religious Thought*, Vol. 46, No. 1,

(Washington: Howard University Press, Winter 1991), 224.
40. J. Kallas, *The Significance of the Synoptic Miracles*, 4th Edition (London: S. P. C. K. 1961), 56. cf. J. Kallas, *Jesus and the Power of Satan*, (Philadelphia: Westminster, 1968), 89 – 92.
41. M. F. Unger, *Demons in the World Today, A Study of Occultism in the Light of God's Word*, (Ibadan: Scripture Union Press, 1986), 2.
42. R. H. Hiers, *Op. cit.* 45. cf. K. W. Clark, "Realized Eschatology," *Journal of Biblical Literature*, Vol. 59, (Philadelphia, Oct. 1940), 377. Clark states: "This is precisely the form, the Syntax; the context makes plain beyond all doubt the sense of pursuit and imminent contact, rather than the idea of an actual conflict."
43. Ibid.
44. Ibid.

6. Evaluation of Evil Spirits, Mysterious Forces and the Control Mechanism in Urhoboland

M.P. Adogbo
Dept. of Religious Studies, Delta State University, Abraka.

Introduction

Among the Urhobo of Delta State, Nigeria, evil spirits and mysterious forces are diverse as could be seen in the day-to-day experience of the people. Evil spirits include primordial spirits and the malignant spirits of the dead members of the social group. These evil spirits are not wanted by the people because they affect directly or indirectly, for worse, every community in Urhoboland. The people believe that they are responsible for the chaos and calamities that plague the entire society. The mysterious powers, on the other hand, are realized by the activities of sorcerers and magicians. They achieve their objectives by manipulating the skills they acquired during contacts with the evil spirits, and also by the use of laws of nature. To what extent has the evil forces influenced the religion and culture of the Urhobo? This is the thesis I strongly wish to present in this paper.

Evil Spirits in Urhobo Traditional Religion

The Urhobo, which is the focus of this work, call the evil spirits, *irhi ri debono*. *Irhi* is plural of *ehri* while *idebono* is calamity or any serious trouble resulting from the activities of evil spirits. When these negative forces are in action, the Urhobo would exclaim, *"Erhi ri' debono ye whe okpetu nana rhe"* (it is an evil spirit that has brought this trouble). Trouble, in this perspective, is called *ese, uko, ukpokogho, odavwini, uboro* and *idebono*. The Urhobo do not have a principal causative agent in the manner of the Biblical Satan as I have shown elsewhere (Adogbo 2003, 27f). The evil spirits in Urhobo religion are autonomous and not under any other spirit, except the supreme Deity. Even when the spirits act together, the notion of *pimus inter pares* (first among equals) does not exit.

The Urhobo believe that the primordial evil spirits are the spirits so created by God. The most notorious ones are *Edjoverivwi* and *Eberowho*. These spirits live in the forest groves, but occasionally come to human habitation to cause trouble. Rituals of afflictions or redressive rituals are offered to these nefarious spirits.

The malignant spirits are the spirits of victims of irregular deaths, such as drowning, suicide, death as a result of thunder, small-pox and death during pregnancy or child-birth. The corpses of victims of these irregular deaths are not accorded the normal funeral rites, and therefore, cannot join the ancestors in the spirit world, called *erivwi*.

The malignant spirits also inhabit the forest groves in Urhoboland. There is a tradition among the Urhobo that if a person commits suicide or dies a mysterious death, as noted above, the victim is buried in the forest. Such forests are called *Awharode* (bad bush). No farming is done in such forests and they are avoided in the Urhobo sacred days; *Edewo* and *Edurhe*.

In an interview with Mr. Albert Isiboge at Orogun in 1986, he narrated his personal experience when he entered *Awharode* on a sacred day. On *Edewo* he went to his farm near an *Awharode*. While he was staking his yams, a voice came from the grove; "*Muophito*" (Put it down). He looked round but saw nothing. He continued his job. Few minutes after, the voice thundered, "put it down." He abandoned the job and raced home. There are other accounts in which the malignant spirits, which are malicious and malevolent, brought sickness and even deaths to people who disobeyed their interdictions.

The belief in witchcraft is a reality among African peoples. The adherents of the traditional religions and even converts to Christianity believe in witchcraft with great tenacity. This belief has not only caused great fears but has also resulted in the death of many people. In spite of the obvious manifestations of witches among African peoples, some foreign anthropologists have argued that witchcraft is an imaginary action. Evans-Pritchard as quoted by Parrinder (1958) has asserted that witchcraft is "an imaginary offence because it is impossible. A witch cannot do what he is supposed to do and in fact has no real existence." He amplifies that "A witch performs no rite, utters no spell, and possesses no medicine. An act of witchcraft is a psychic act."

The above description of witchcraft is astonishing and its justification will be doubted by most Africans who believe that witches fly about at night and meet in secret conclaves such as iroko, silk-cotton trees or in the forest groves. The witches are associated with birds, such as nightjars, owl, and bats, especially vampires, which fly about in the night. They suck the blood of their victims until they die.

The Urhobo, as well as some ethnic groups in Africa, believe that witches are generally women. In most cases, it is hereditary as parents pass it on to their children at the embryo stage. There are other cases when witches put a special spiritual substance into food, so that the person who eats the substance becomes a witch. There are also instances when some human spirits reject the spirit substance, even if it is eaten. This looks like a kind of natural immunity. In the case of family inheritance, the spirits of some people within the family do not succumb to the manipulations of witches. This is essentially an issue, which relates to destiny.

The concept of destiny (*urhievwe* or *otarhe*) is very important in the religion and culture of the Urhobo. It is believed that before one is born into the physical world, his *erhi* (spirit) would appear before an assembly of the ancestral spirits to declare his destiny. It is during this occasion that some people declare that they would not join the witches when they are born into the physical world. A destiny, which is so declared, may not be altered, especially if the person lives to the dictates of God who sealed the destiny with a print on both palms. There are isolated cases when the destinies of some people are altered on account of their irresponsibility.

The Urhobo believe that witches meet at night in their covens or convents. In the process of the meeting, members make contributions from their immediate families; this could be a prominent person in the family of the witch. The donation of such high rank individual would earn the witch who made the donation a very high position. In other cases, they donate their children, and husbands or wives, depending on the sex of the witch. As the victims are transformed into animals and killed in the coven, the action happens simultaneously in the physical world. The witches do not succeed in all cases for the reasons already stated above. Witches also punish their victims with illness, which does not respond to orthodox treatment in government hospitals. In such cases, the victims patronize mediums, traditional doctors, and in recent years, spiritualists in the Pentecostal churches.

The Urhobo believe that witches are responsible for the economic and social woes that plague the various communities. They negatively influence the economic potentialities of the people. This they do by causing heavy rains that destroy farmlands and also protracted droughts, which result in crop failure. In a nutshell, the witch is accused when the people are faced with any calamity.

Like the primordial evil spirits and the malignant spirits of the dead, witchcraft activities are associated with forest groves and big trees. The people believe that the trees or forests are transformed into magnificent buildings where they carry out their nefarious activities. Many other ethnic groups in the world share this belief that forest groves are the home of evil spirits. For example, in the Ancient Near East, forest groves are regarded as homes of sacred spirits. Thus at Shechem, the Oak of Moreh, was an important sacred shrine where the native Canaanites made sacrifices to their deities. It became the first encampment of Abraham when he arrived in the land of Canaan. Here God promised to give him and his descendants all the land of Canaan. To commemorate this important event, Abraham built there an altar to the LORD. (Gen. 12: 6-7).

In Urhoboland, the community *edjo* (divinities) are usually made in thick forest groves. This could be a war divinity or any divinity made for the progress of the community. In some communities, it is taboo for women and children to enter the forests.

Apart from the evil spirits noted above, there are other mystical forces, which cause people to walk on fire without harm, lie on thorns on nails, to change to animals (lycanthropy), powers that enable experts to see into secrets, hidden information of the past or the future. These forces have affected almost every Urhobo person, either positively or negatively. These powers are manifested in magic, medicine and sorcery.

Magic can be defined as an attempt by man to tap and control supernatural powers or resources of the universe for his own benefit. James Frazer in his book, *The Golden Bough* (1900), made a distinction between magic and religion. He observes that man, in the absence of scientific technology seek to control nature with the use of magic. He placed magic at a lower intellectual level than the belief in personal deities. On evolutionary grounds, he placed magic as the forerunner of religion. The motto of magic is, "My will be done" while that of religion is, "Thy will be done." Magic is generally considered under "good magic" and "bad magic". The good magic is accepted and admired by society.

The good magic is used in the treatment of diseases, counteracting misfortunes and destroying evil powers of witches and sorcerers. Good magic is produced in the form of rings, charms, amulets etc. It could also be used for the protection of the family and community. The evil magic, on the other hand, involves the practice of tapping and using evil forces to do harm to human beings or their property. In this "black magic" parts of human body or property could be used to work evil against the victim.

Magic operates on two principles namely, homeopathic magic and contagious magic. Homeopathic magic acts on the law of similarity that "like produces like." This involves the belief that what happens to an object which looks like another will affect the latter. Thus a doll or an image could be made to represent an enemy. Whatever that is done to the doll affects the enemy. The contagious or sympathetic magic is based on the principle that using a part of a thing may affect the whole. This homeopathic or sympathetic magic has been used extensively by sorcerers to cause harm to their enemies in various parts of Africa.

Sorcery involves the use of poisonous ingredients, which are either put into food or manipulated in such a way that they can kill or harm someone or destroy property. A person who uses this "bad magic" is called a sorcerer. In African societies, sorcerers are not only hated but they are also feared. They send bees, snakes, crocodiles and other animals to attack their enemies or carry diseases to them. They spit and direct the spittle with secret incantations and use of ventriloquism to go and harm their victims. They invoke evil spirits to attack or possess their enemies. It is as a result of the evil practices of the sorcerers that all incurable and protracted illnesses are attributed to them in Urhobo traditional cosmology.

As a result of the evil machinations of sorcerers, people resort to medicine men, mediums and diviners to supply them the necessary cure or protection against their evil actions. The protective medicines are in the form of charms, rings, and leather belts, pots with prepared concoctions and mystical ropes, which are hung at the entrance of doors, compounds or the village. The cultural affirmation of this logic is that the good use of the mystical powers could counteract the evil ones. It is by this philosophy that the hopes of the Urhobo for a better and progressive society are sustained.

Control Mechanisms
(i). *Redressive or Rituals of Affliction*
Redressive ritual exists to redress a calamity or an affliction, which has brought about a crisis in the affairs of a social group. This could be in the form of epidemics or a protracted drought or rainfall, which results in large-scale destruction of farmlands and property. It may be a sickness or affliction that has befallen an individual who, thereupon, becomes the symbol of tension within the community. After series of investigations, the medium or diviner would reveal the social and spiritual structures that are responsible for the problem. They would proffer

possible solution, which may be in the form of rituals to make the hidden tensions explicit and in the process restore the *status quo ante*.

Rituals of this nature are called *izobo* among the Urhobo. It is also called *ese* by some Urhobo polities, especially the Ewhu people. The generic term, *izobo* implies that a spirit has manifested and therefore offering be made to appease the *erhi ri'debono* (the evil spirit). The Okuama people of Ewhu polity would say, *ese sare, egbi ri ze izobo vwo ke* (a spirit has manifested, an offering be made to it). Here, *ese*, which is *izobo*, is used for the evil spirit. This is the problem of language which a novice may not be able to interpret.

Izobo among the Urhobo is an offering presented to spirits, especially the evil spirits of the land to enlist their co-operation. The *izobo* is offered with the hope of restoring normalcy between man and the spirit beings. The essence of *izobo* is that whatever that is offered to the spirit could either be accepted or rejected.

The medium identifies the problem and recommends the appropriate ritual elements for the offering. In some cases, the mediums or a designated individual or group performs the ritual at a road junction, usually at the outskirts of the town. A place where two roads meet is called *aderha* in the Urhobo language. All such meeting points, either inside the community or at the outskirts are sacred and have great religious signification in Urhoboland.

Aderha is the meeting point of the living and the spirits of the departed members of the community as well as all primordial spirits. In their visits to the town, the spirits, witches and all evil forces pass through the crossroads. In short, they are the busiest points in the traditional society. It is on this logical consideration that the road junctions are regarded as the most appropriate sites for sacrifices to evil spirits. This explanation seems an over simplification or personification of the ritual process. What is certain is that the ritual practices are mystical in nature and cannot be fully explained or comprehended by the ordinary man.

The *aderha* is the meeting point of human beings and the malignant spirits, which are not wanted in the town. The people believe that on the appointed day for the offering, both parties meet at the crossroad, being a neutral zone. Here the i*zobo* is performed. It could take one of several forms.

(ii). *Pollution and Purification rites*
In the Urhobo traditional religion and cultural setting, it is absolutely impossible for any individual to absolve himself from the various prohibitions. Taboo, pollution and purification rites are essential elements in the traditional religion and culture of the people. Taboo is

the development of a sense of what is to be done or not to be done. This has enhanced the people's belief in absolute standard of right and wrong.

Taboos regulate the moral and social life of the people. They are legitimized by religious sanctions. According to Bouquet, (1962:52), " thus taboos, ... are the religious models which are played with by the race in its childhood, but which are not idle things, since they prepare it for the more serious business of adult spiritual [and cultural/social] life, just as the bricks and dolls of boys and girls prepare them for handicraft and motherhood".

Durkheim (1946), provides a classification, which enhances the enforcement of taboos. In his view, all known religious beliefs, whether simple or complex, present one common characteristic. They presuppose a classification or division of the world into two domains, the one containing all that is sacred, and the other, all that is profane. The sacred things are par excellence that, which the profane should not touch, and must not touch with impunity. In this capacity, sacred things are those, which interdictions are applied and which must remain at a distance from the profane.

If a person breaks a taboo or prohibition, pollution occurs. The breach of religious taboos is abomination among the Urhobo. The state of pollution and the threat of supernatural sanctions can only be removed by purification rites. The Urhobo traditional religion demands a pious observance of the social and religious codes. It is generally believed that the moral codes are dictated by the divinities from time to time. Even if a new law is made in respect of an ethical code, legitimization is sought from the divinities by the pouring of libation to them. In this regard, the divinities, especially the ancestors, are particularly significant.

The breach of any of these prohibitions automatically puts the offender in a state of pollution. The evil spirits are always the first to take action against the offender as they look for the slightest opportunity to interfere in the affairs of men. By the pollution, the offender loses the natural and acquired immunity. Under this condition, the offender must not approach the altars of the divinities or venture into the sacred forests. Also, he must not take part in any collective or communal ritual until the necessary purification rites are performed.

Purification rites

One may be tempted to breach one or several other prohibitions. To restore the *status quo*, various kinds of purification rites have been introduced. The nature of the rites depends on the degree and severity of the offence. The state of defilement, which results from infringement of minor prohibitions, like hatred of family members, stealing of fish or animals from neighbor's traps are less severe. These minor prohibitions may not pose grave threat to the cosmic and social order. For this reason, the rites are minor and the costs of items for the purification rites are less expensive.

In the case of pollution, which results in a serious abomination affecting the entire community, elaborate rituals are performed. Animals, birds and various food items may be needed. This is essentially, what we have designated in this work as redressive ritual. It is a common tradition in Urhobo religion and culture that all the members of the community must offer redressive or rituals of afflictions. Below are the accounts of interviews conducted on this subject all over Urhoboland.

In an interview with J. Riesa at Ughelli in 1994, he narrated that redressive rituals are common phenomena among the Egbo-Uhurie people of Jeremi polity. He gave an eyewitness account of *izobo* offered by the people of his town. According to the source, the people of Egbo-Uhurie were beset by a serious health problem resulting from a protracted epidemic disease, which was identified as measles. Both orthodox and traditional healing methods were used but the epidemic persisted. The elders of the town consulted an oracle and it was established that an evil spirit was responsible. The diviner identified the ritual elements that were required for the *izobo*.

Then every household in the town was asked to contribute any food item, such as plantain, eggs, cassava, pepper, etc. These were assembled in the community hall. From this point designated men, women, boys and girls were sent to carry the ritual items to the outskirts of the town to perform the offering. He explained that one significant feature of the offering is that all the food items that were contributed were substandard and not fit for human consumption. They were made up of rotten cassava, fish, yam and premature plantain. The reason for this was that evil spirits do not deserve any good sacrifice as other divinities. This is consequent on the fact that the people do not want the evil spirits, because of their unwholesome and nefarious activities, which usually cause tension and woes in the community. If they were presented with good food they would be making regular visits to the town. Urhobo people are of the opinion that good gifts are to be given to the people they love. The evil spirits are enemies and, therefore, do not require any hospitality for which they are known. As we have noted earlier, they make efforts to keep the evil spirits out of human habitation.

The elements, which the people contributed were deposited at the site with a prayer that the evil spirits should keep out of the town and never come again. According to Riesa, these efforts do not keep the spirits permanently out of the town. After a while, they return and the same process is repeated, but may vary depending on the demands of the spirit that has manifested or the intensity of the disaster.

The riverine communities in Urhoboland also perform the rituals of affliction. The people of Okuama, Gbaregolo and Furukama offer communal rituals at the beginning of the dry season when the floods have receded. The women collect several food items and move from one end of the town (usually up-stream) to the other side (down stream). After several prayers had been said for the safety of the entire people and requests that the evil spirits should keep out of the community, the women threw the elements into the river in turns. On the day such rituals are performed in Okuama, no boats are allowed to come on shore in the town. They may do so at the outskirts.

It is clear from the above examples that no specific procedure or laid down rules are followed in the performance of the rituals of affliction among the Urhobo. In the case of pollution, which results in abomination, elaborate rituals are performed. Animals, such as sheep, goats and fowls are commonly used. This offering may take the form scapegoatism. At the site of the purification rites, the sins of the offender are mystically transferred into the animal victim. It may then be killed or left to stray as the spirit demands.

The underlying knowledge of the various rituals connected with scapegotism is that the sins committed by the persons are taken away from the head of the offender and transferred to the animal, which now becomes the scapegoat. The rituals of affliction are in the form of propitiation or expiation, which are directed towards a set objective by the community. In some cases they are performed by individual whose deeds have become a source of great worry for the community.

Conclusion

I have attempted an evaluation of the spiritual forces in Urhobo traditional religion and culture in this paper. The people believe that evil spirits and mysterious forces are responsible for the chaos and calamities that plague the society from time to time. Thus several control mechanisms, which are aimed at maintaining the equilibrium, have been put in place. These rituals of afflictions and purification rites have been thoroughly discussed. Whereas the ritual of affliction is aimed at addressing a calamity which has brought about a crisis in the affairs of the social group, the purification rites are performed when there is a breach that poses grave threat to the cosmic and social order. The paper established that the belief in the existence of the evil spirits and forces have given authenticity and legitimacy to the activities of

References

Adogbo, M.P. (2003) "The Search for The Biblical Satan in Urhobo Traditional Religion". *The Nigerian Journal of Theology* Vol. 17.

Bouquet, A.C. (1962), *Comparative Religion*, Harmondsworth: Penguin Books Ltd.

Durkheim, E, (1946 trans. J. Swain, 1961) *The Elementary Forms of Religious life*, New York: The Fortress Press.

Frazer, J.C. (1922) *The Golden Bough*, London.

Parrinder, E. G. (1958), *Witch-Craft: European and Africa*, London: Faber & Faber.

7. The Meaning & Significance of Festivals in Traditional African Culture & Life*

Chris I. Ejizu
Dept. of Religious & Cultural Studies, University of Port Harcourt.

Introduction

Great and valiant Ofori
I am off to Abirem Akyem,
I am going to the stool house
Where room encloses room
King of hosts
Who is ever sought for an ally in battle
Benevolent great killer
Vanguard amongst equals
Unconquerable one,
Dread of the old and the young
Grandson of Ofori of the Asona clan
He that balances the keg of gun-powder upon his head
And somersaults over the flames
He that bends the sword with ease
Out, and come with me
Out, and come with me!
(Opoku 1970: 10 -11)

The foregoing thrilling words resonate from the talking drum of the Chief's principal drummer. He summons the Chief and his entourage to the *Adae* festival of the Akan, Ghana. Not only among the Akan, but all through sub-Saharan Africa, festivals are very popular and recurrent events in traditional life and culture. Whether among sedentary land-cultivating peoples, like the Idoma and Yoruba of Nigeria, or highly itinerant peoples like the Wolof and Masai of Senegal and Kenya respectively, festivals marking one event or the other, are favourite and frequent occurrence. People celebrate significant events including critical stages in the human life-cycle, or historical landmarks in the annals of a group. Festivals are equally organised to mark significant stages in the agricultural or occupational calendar, or purely as religious act of reverence to certain prominent deity or nature force that is believed to underpin some vital life-interest of a group.

The *ihejioku/ahanjoku* festival among the traditional Igbo (held annually in honour of the nature force, *ahanjoku/njoku ji*, believed to be responsible for yam, the prince of all traditional Igbo agricultural products) is a good example. The cheer multiplicity of these festivals in traditional African communities indicates the considerable time people spend on them. The elaborate preparation usually made to ensure their success, suggests the tremendous resources people commit to their celebration.

A festival, by definition, is any special occasion, observance or celebration which may be religious or secular in nature, and that is generally marked by merry-making, performance of music and the like. Traditional Africans are no different from other groups of humankind in celebrating publicly significant episodes in their individual and communal life-experience. In both traditional and modern societies, people commemorate in different ways, a variety of prominent events in their history. Countries annually mark their national day with elaborate fanfare. The French in 1989 celebrated with remarkable pageantry the second centenary of the all-important event of their national history; the French Revolution. The Chinese and some other Asian countries continue annually to mark the inception of their traditional new year with rich festival. For hundreds of millions of Christians and Muslims, the feasts of Christmas and *Id-el-Malud* are times for extraordinary celebration. They are for the two religious bodies occasions for joyful re-enactment of the important religious facts of the birth of Jesus Christ and the Prophet Muhammad respectively.

As the title of this paper suggests, I propose to focus specifically on the meaning and significance of festivals in traditional African culture and life. I hope to argue that in traditional African cultural background, the real meaning and ultimate significance of festivals lie not in the social or economic aspect, but in the indigenous cosmology of the different groups. As a unified perception of the universe and reality as a whole, explained by a system of concepts which order the natural and social rhythms, African traditional cosmology is basically holistic and sacred. The meaning and implication of individual festivals are imbedded within that fundamental perception which the different groups cultivated as an integral aspect of their total life-experience (including the ecological and socio-historical aspects). I plan to embark on a detailed explanation of the issues after I shall have disposed of the fundamental matter of classification and structure of festivals. It is pertinent to point out that for traditional Africans, festivals are essentially symbolic performance. As such, they stand for, and re-present to people a multiplicity of things at the same time. The sacred and transcendental centre, however, remains the firm and ultimate anchor of traditional festivals.

Classification of Festivals
A number of criteria could be used to classify traditional African festivals. It is possible, for example, to sub-divide them simply with the factor of participation into *general participation festivals and, limited participation festivals*. As

the descriptions suggest, a general participation festival "is characterized by a large group celebration, while a limited participation festival is restricted to more exclusive groups" (Anambra State Cultural Unit, 1977: 9).

One could also borrow the scheme of R. Pilgrim (1978: 65), and simply categorize African traditional festivals into:

(a) *Festivals associated with ecological cycles*
This class incorporates festivals whose timing, nature and intent are closely associated with cycles of the natural order, such as festivals that commemorate planetary movements and seasonal changes; planting, harvesting, hunting, fishing and animal cycles.

(b) *Festivals of non-ecological liturgical calendars*
These are usually festivals of specific religious character that follow a regular, cyclic pattern of repetition but are not primarily linked to the cycles of the natural universe.

(c) *Festivals of the human cycle*
As the name implies, these are festivals marking some crucial stages of the human life-cycle – "rites of passage" – like birth, initiation, marriage and funeral.

(d) *Occasional festivals*

These cover festivals which do nor necessarily follow any regular cycle of repetition but are staged "on demand", whenever necessary.

There are numerous examples of each of the types in different African societies. A wide range of traditional festivals are, for example, connected with the lunar cycle, the agricultural and other occupational seasons. Some communities of the north-western Igbo sub-culture area like Nnewi, have an annual festival for maidens known as *Isi-Ebili* in which moonlight displays by young girls form an integral part. The festival is usually, therefore, scheduled to coincide with the period of full moon in the months of March and April. The *Ngbegbengbe* festival of the Andoni people of Rivers State is celebrated annually during the rainy season, around the month of June, to mark the end of one occupational season and the beginning of another. The *Homowo* of the Ga people of southern Ghana (Opoku 1970), the *Edjo* of the Urhobo, (Delta State, Nigeria), the *Ihejioku/Ahiajioku/Afia-olu* of the Igbo, and the *Fungu* of the Andoni community of Rivers State, are all festivals of the agricultural cycle.

In addition to festivals closely associated with the movement of the universe and major occupations of people, most traditional African groups have their respective calendars of regular liturgical feasts. These are often in honour of ancestors, various deities, nature and cosmic forces acknowledged by the people. Some of the festivals are minor (observed by a limited group in the entire community), while others are major (observed by the entire community and involving elaborate celebration). The *Egungun* and *Oro* of the Yoruba, the *Duen* of the Kalabari, the *Ekwe* of the Andoni and the *Adae* the Akan are all major festivals in honour of the ancestral spirits among the respective groups. While the *Ikwu-aru* and *Ajachi//Ilo-chi* of some Igbo communities and the *Molimo* of the Mbuti people of Zaire, are examples of festivals dedicated to specific deities of various groups.

Festivals of the human cycle, especially those marking major initiation into title–societies are very prominent and widespread. They include the prestigious *Ichi-Ozo* and *Ugwu Ogerinya* of the Igbo, the Yoruba naming ceremony known as *Ikomojade*, the initiation into manhood, *Poro* and *Sande* of Liberia and Sierra Leone respectively, the *Nkang'a* for Ndembu girls of Zambia. Funerals of people who died at ripe old age and in "good" standing (i.e. not in circumstances infringing any of the taboos of society), are occasions of elaborate and often expensive celebration. Examples of occasional festivals would include celebrations to mark the achievement of one special feat or another, such as victory in warfare, the killing of a big animal like a leopard, elephant or crocodile. In recent times, the return of an illustrious son or daughter, spectacular success in sports, the winning of an election, or success at an important football match, could also afford people occasion for celebration and full-scale festival. The Abonema people, Rivers State, celebrate annually around June, their liberation from Biafran soldiers by the Federal Nigerian army with a rich festival. In Igboland, on the other hand, the return of Chief Emeka Odumegwu Ojukwu in 1983, after thirteen years of exile in Ivory Coast erupted into a major occasional festival. In addition to huge crowds of people that gathered in many towns to welcome him back, there were widespread celebrations in parts of the region as well as display of such celebrated traditional masquerades as *Ijele*, *Ekpe, Iri-Agha/Ikpilikpe-Ogu, Egbenu-Oba* and *Abiadike*.

One final observation that should be noted about the foregoing classification is, that the scheme is only an analytical tool. In real life, traditional Africans do not classify their festivals into types as such. Rather, each society, based on its total context of life (ecology, occupation, socio-historical experience, vital interests), evolved a calendar that encompasses and caters for key aspects of life of its people. Festivals punctuate the different phases of normal life from year to year. Leading groups and persons, including elders and ritual experts (who are supposed to be custodians of traditional norms and customs, as part of their duty of maintaining social order), ensure that the sequence of ritual events and festivals is religiously followed.

Structure of Festivals

Given the wide variety of festivals that exist and coupled with the characteristic oral nature of the indigenous cultural background of most traditional African groups, one can only legitimately talk of a loose kind of structure for traditional festivals. Even in the same society there are festivals that occur regularly like the *Adae* festival of the Akan and the *Afia-Olu* festival of some Igbo groups. There are others that are celebrated at long intervals (e.g. once every seven, ten or even twenty-five years), for example, *Mgbuli, Asala* and *Ikwu-Aru* among some Igbo groups and *Ujingbek* among the Andoni. Similarly, some festivals last only for a day, while some others are drawn-out for upwards of one week or more. Still, in some societies, there are festivals whose celebrations are graduated (sometimes, by way of age sets, or gender), to a climax involving the entire community. In spite of the diversity of types, a certain kind of general structure could still be discerned.

Most festivals usually have the following three-fold structural pattern:

i. Preparatory stage
ii. Actual celebration
iii. Conclusion and Dispersal

Given the importance of festivals among traditional Africans, people need time to prepare for their successful celebration. The period of preparation varies. Sometimes, it is determined by the scope of the festival, particularly for festivals that occur after some relatively long intervals. There are generally remote and proximate preparations. The arrangements usually include the performance of some requisite rituals, as well as provision of things that will be used for the celebrations.

Among the Igbo, remote preparations for such festivals as the royal *Ofalla* in many communities would involve the consultation of diviners to ascertain the disposition of the ancestors and deities. People would also like to ascertain the kind of preventive and purificatory sacrifices to be offered to predispose the ancestors and other spirit beings positively. At times, the making of new symbol objects for the celebration is commissioned and new structures are erected in the festival arena. Invariably, the arrangement would entail the accumulation of wealth for the procurement of all kinds of materials to be used including foodstuff, drinks, animals, accoutrement, and gifts. Various groups might undertake to learn new dances for display on the occasion.

Proximate preparations generally take the form of tidying up and decorating homes, shrines and public places, offering of preventing or purificatory sacrifices to ward-off any malevolent forces that might threaten a successful celebration, or to put the participants in a proper moral disposition. Opoku reports that among the Akan, *Memenda Dapaa* is the name of the Saturday preceding the Sunday *Adae* (ancestral festival). It is a day for all kinds of preparation;

> *Foodstuffs, firewood, water, drinks, chicken, sheep, eggs and the articles required for the celebration of the Adae are brought home on the Dapaa. On the Adae days, no work or travel may be done except duties connected with the celebration. ... Villages, towns and wells and footpaths leading to them are also cleaned. There is much activity at the chief's house. Attendants and stool-carriers scrub the white stools and calabashes needed for the Adae celebration. The horn blowers and state drummers also busy themselves tuning the instruments which they will use to usher in the Adae in the evening of the Dapaa. At sundown, when all the preparations are complete, the drummers assemble at the chief's house and drum till late in the night* (1970: 8).

The stage of actual celebration is generally ushered in some formal way by many traditional African groups. The performance of some rituals at the shrine of the deities in whose honour the festivals are staged is the most prevailing manner of declaring events open. At times, a ritual sacrifice is made at individual family shrines led by heads of families. Such customary gifts like kola nuts, white chalk (*nzu*), and libations are made to patron spirits at their altar or through the medium of their symbol objects. Usually the officiating expert communicates the special intentions for the celebration to the spirits in prayer. Animal victims are then slaughtered at their altar and the meat used as part of the items for food.

Other ways of formally ushering in festivals in traditional African societies include the firing of cannons/guns, the early patrol of some special masquerades to public shrines or festival grounds. The sounding of the talking drum or the *Ikoro* (wooden gong) is equally common in many West African societies. The lines of the talking drum (text cited at the beginning of this paper), of the Chief's principal drummer among the Akan of Ghana is a typical example. The divine drummer, as he is otherwise called rises early in the morning of the *Adae* festival and sounds the drum. At first, he greets the chief and recounts his marvelous deeds. After an interval of about an hour, he sounds his instruments again, this time to summon the chief and his *entourage* to the stool-house in which the people's symbol objects of the ancestors are stored.

A striking feature of the celebration of most festivals in traditional societies is the preparation of local delicacies. Such special menus and dishes differ from place to place. Breadfruit *(Ukwa)*, cocoyam fou-fou *(Utara-Ede)*, a special class of sauce *(Oke-Ofe* or *Mkpum)*, are favorite dishes for festivals among many north-western Igbo communities like Umudioka, Ogidi and Nnewi. At Umuezeaka Mgbo, the *Esheke* dish which is specially prepared with fried melon topped with dry meat of grass-cutter is for the Itutara festival which celebrates the initiation of the adolescent girls in preparation for the traditional marriage. In Udi, on the other hand, the *Iheaneke* festival which marks the initiation of young boys is noted for the *Ighu* dish which is prepared with fried crickets.

Festivals are occasions for lavish eating and drinking. From the homes where family members and guests are entertained, celebrations gradually move to public arenas and village squares. People converge in large numbers, even from neighbouring communities to enjoy dances and masquerade displays which form an integral part of many African traditional festivals. In the case of the *Aso* festival (a new yam festival in Nkalagu), people gather to watch wrestling competition between villages with the accompanying drumming and dancing. In Aguleri, for the Ikenga festival, people assemble in the central village shrine/square to watch the display of the richly decorated *Ikenga a*rt symbol *(Ugonachonma),* as well as to present all babies born in the community in the course of the year to the patron spirit of achievement, *Ikenga* during the annual *Ime Ikenga* festival.

Traditional festivals are normally brought to a close in a number of ways. In some cases, festivals conclude with the leader of the community simply making some pronouncement. But the prevalent manner is by the offering of some ritual sacrifice by ritual experts at the shrine of the particular deity that has been the major focus of attention during the celebration. The motive of such a sacrifice is generally propitiatory. At times, the concluding sacrifice is accompanied by the imposition of some ritual restriction on the community. People then disperse to their respective homes and occupations. The different objects and outfits that were used for the celebration are stored away for safe-keeping.

Cosmological Foundation of Festivals

The indigenous African understanding of the universe and reality as a whole is sacred and holistic. Time is thought to move in a cyclical fashion as the seasons of the year, the sun, the moon and natural events repeat themselves in an interminable way. Mircea Eliade refers to this repetitive order in nature as "The myth of eternal return". The different levels of space are perceived as inhabited. Human beings and the rest of the visible order occupy the earth surface. While invisible beings, including ancestral spirits and patron deities as well as cosmic forces are believed to dominate the invisible world.

The reality and dynamic involvement of spiritual beings in events and activities in the universe, including the movement of the seasons, the provision of rain, fertility, etc, is a fundamental item of belief of every African indigenous religion adherents. Deities and important mythical beings are believed to have ordained certain normative patterns. They had assisted in establishing important cultural institutions, as well as revealed to people specific ways of engaging in such key professions and trades like blacksmithing, hunting, farming, fishing, medicine-making, etc., in the mythical past. (The myths of origin of different African groups spell out the details in various ways). Patron spirits and deities are thought to be intricately involved in the general fortunes of human beings. They continue to undergird various life-interests and occupations associated with them.

Important aspects of life are, therefore, integrated in this fundamental view of reality, that is the traditional cosmology of the different indigenous African groups.

For the land-cultivating traditional Igbo, for example, the earth on which people depend for their livelihood, is deified. The powerful spirit being which is supposed to be the patron deity, *Ala*, is equally the underpinner of fertility and the custodian of morality. Agriculture has its own spirit-protectors, especially yam, the prince of all Igbo agricultural products and the focal centre of the traditional calendar. *Ihejioku/Ahiajioku/Njoku ji* is the yam cosmic force and special supernatural ally of the traditional farmer. While for the diviner, the traditional medicine-man and other gifted practitioners, *Agwu* is the patron spirit-force that enlightens and helps successful practice.

Traditional Africans clearly endeavour to live their lives in close contact and partnership, so to speak, with their patron spirit beings and benevolent deities. By conforming their various life-experiences to the normative patterns believed to have been revealed by the gods in mythical past, people are convinced that they are able to attract divine favour, and thereby maintain the delicate relationship between humans and the invisible spiritual beings. Thus, they ensure the maximum success of their earthly life.

Most traditional festivals, no doubt, are closely tied to ecological, occupational and human cycles. Their real meaning and deep significance lie within the vital context of the same fundamental cosmology of the people. Individual festivals may be linked to certain significant event or activity in people's lives. They may occur at a period of time the community considers more convenient in their occupational calendar, for example, the harvest time (when materials for feasting would normally be readily available, the volume of work lessened, and the need for recreation much more felt). Or, they may be related to a need a group may feel to re-enact symbolically on regular basis, certain dominant motifs of their particular culture, for example, achievement among the Igbo. These elements and circumstances are important in the idea of festivals among traditional Africans. Ultimately however, the deities and cosmic beings believed to undergird special areas of life and interest, have a pride of place in the celebrations. Traditional Africans organize their festivals to thank, appease or propitiate their spiritual patrons and partners with whom people's lives and fortunes are intricately bound. Spiritual beings and deities are believed to ultimately invest traditional African festivals with their real meaning and significance.

Not surprisingly, therefore, many traditional African festivals simply go by the same names as the deities and spiritual forces in whose honour they are staged. For instance, among the indigenous Igbo, the new yam festival is commonly known as *Ime Ihejioku/Ahiajioku/Njoku*. At Abatete, *Omaliko*, the name of the major divinity of the people is also the name of the annual festival. The same goes for *Nwafor* festival in Ogidi, *Mkpukpa* festival in Umudioka, while in Aguleri, *Ime Ikenga* is the name of the festival of the cosmic force responsible for achievement. Furthermore, the fact that most traditional festivals are prefaced by different types of ritual performances including divination, preventive sacrifice, ritual procession, or inaugurated with thanksgiving offerings, staged in sacred arena and shrine of relevant deities as well as concluded, just as they began, on a religious note, are clearly indicative of where the pendulum falls, that is where people place the accent, in such festivals. Neither should it be forgotten that the appearance of masquerades, which is a striking feature of many traditional festivals, is supposed to be concrete dramatization of the symbolic presence in the festivals of ancestral and other patron spirits. In the appearance of such masquerades, the gods are perceived as guests.

Multi-dimensional Characteristic of Festivals

Festivals in general are multi-dimensional in character, involving the emotional, aesthetic, social, economic, religious and other facets of life. Different explanations have tended to play up one or the other of the aspects depending on the intellectual hue of the author. Scholars like Josef Pieper emphasize the importance of leisure as a precondition for the successful festival. Emile Durkheim on the other hand, accentuates the collective effervescence or exuberant movements which mark festivals. Robin Horton (who has since been followed by E.P. Modum, 1978), describes Kalabari festivals with the title, "The Gods as Guests" (Nigerian Magazine, Special edition, 1960).

Festivals remain by their nature multidimensional in character. They have significance for virtually every aspects of life of the community in the traditional African. They have implications for individuals, as well as groups and the society at large. Their significance ranges from the psychological, recreational, through social and economic, to the religious facets of life. We shall proceed to discus their implications for these dimensions.

Psychological: Festivals in general are of immense psychological importance to human beings as individuals and groups. Scholars including Durkheim, had actually referred to them as periods of "collective effervescence" (or "collective euphoria", in the words of Callois), often marked by paroxysms (Durkheim 1936: 426). Festivals provide people freer periods for the expression of pent-up emotions. In some festivals, deliberate effort is made through such media like masked figures, talking drums recitals, mimetic dances, etc., to criticize and satirise the unacceptable behaviour of members of the group. This is a common phenomenon associated with the *Ulaga* masquerade, the *Udu* figure in the *Ekpe* ensemble, or even the *Abaigbo* dance recitals of the Mbaise area of Igboland.

Given also the rigid norms and numerous taboos that characterise ethical life in traditional African society, the period of relaxed control on the behaviour of the people which traditional festivals provide, is of considerable psychological effect. Furthermore, many of the traditional festivals which symbolically celebrate certain key values and motifs, have an additional function of mobilising individuals and groups towards a greater commitment to the pursuit of such ideas. This is precisely the case in such celebrations as the festival which marks the outing ceremony of the *Ozo* title initiate. The prestige and honour that form an integral part of it, no doubt, challenge the uninitiated to work hard in order to achieve the necessary wealth required to procure such expensive title. In a similar vein in the traditional Igbo background, both the *Ewu-Ukwu* ceremony of Mbaise and the *Ahia Onu-nwa* of Ngwa seek to induce female members to embrace child-bearing with joy, the difficulties entailed notwithstanding.

a) *Recreational Aspect*

The recreational significance of festivals is equally high and closely related in importance to the psychological feature. Leisure is very crucial to balanced human growth, health and development. It is a central aspect of African traditional festivals. People usually suspend occupations that afford them a leaving in order to relax and attend to the lighter and more aesthetic aspects of life. Leisure, which is part of festivals, provide people the opportunity to engage in such imaginative activities like carving, weaving, music, story-telling, dancing and other creative activities. People also have the opportunity to contemplate the benevolence of the gods and ancestors. They also afford people the time to renew their energy for more determined pursuits towards making an overall success of their life. Interestingly, most communities of the Niger Delta whose main occupation is fishing, hold their most important festivals in the months of June to August. That is traditionally the holiday period for such communities. People do not usually embark on serious fishing in those due to heavy rainfall.

(b) *Social and Economic Aspects*
African traditional festivals also have significant implications for the social, political and economic domains. Festivals are periods when social ties and political loyalties are reaffirmed and strengthened. At family and other levels of society, people more readily discharge their respective roles in order to ensure the success of the celebration. Children generally obey their

parents more readily in the hope of inducing their kindness. Parents on the other hand, are more mindful for the general well-being of their children and wards. They try to please their children by purchasing new dresses as well as sponsoring their children's initiation into masquerade society, or in performing new dances. People exchange gifts and renew their friendship and other social ties.

Festivals are also periods when communities achieve peace and harmony more easily. Given the usually relaxed atmosphere that prevails during such celebrations, people are more disposed to resolve old scores and forgive their fellows any wrongs they might have done to them.

Traditional festivals are periods *par excellence* for socialisation. In the moonlight plays, story-telling sessions, public gathering and displays that mark such celebrations, young members of society are taught the traditional wisdom, norms and patterns of acceptable moral behaviour of the community. The different public rituals and dramatic performances that feature also ensure that the culture of the people is kept alive and successfully transmitted to successive generations. Some festivals, more than others highlight, certain social and political values. The *Ofalla* festival in many Igbo communities deliberately sets out to renew the important bond of relationship between the people and their traditional rulers. The *Ilo Chi* festival plays up the sacred duty of honour which children owe to their mothers. Finally, in contemporary times, festivals have become for many groups the great occasion to mobilise the people for one major communal development or another (e.g. rural electrification, pipe-borne water, school building).

Economically, the lavish celebration which mark festivals involve considerable exchange of goods, money and services among the people. Festivals usually entail extra financial expenditure in foodstuffs, clothes, cosmetics, etc. money is also spent to purchase animals like goat, sheep, and cow. New outfit for masquerades and uniform for dances involve money as well. Certain festivals are purposely organized as a forum for the display of wealth, such as Ichi Ozo and Ichi Ekwe for men and women in Igboland respectively.

c) *Religious Aspect*

With the traditional cosmology as their anchor, the religious significance of African traditional festivals should not be difficult to figure out. Traditional Africans believe that spirit beings and cosmic forces underpin all vital aspects of life. Against that background festivals are seen primarily as acts of worship offered periodically to such spiritual beings, to thank them for their protection and benevolent intervention in people's lives. Apart from being occasion for honour and thanksgiving, festivals make it possible for people to reaffirm and strengthen their beliefs and relationship with their supernatural allies.

Furthermore, since traditional festivals are largely sacred in character and are often reenacted in sacred atmosphere, they serve as avenues for people to hallow various facets of life. For example, festivals associated with the ecological cycle often serve as means to sacralise the seasons of nature and occupational interests of people, as well as the fruits of human labour on which people depend for livelihood.

Finally, traditional festivals are powerful communicators of people's religious and cultural traditions. Their regular reenactment helps to keep rituals associated with them alive. At, neighbouring groups decide to learn certain displays like masquerades and dance performances they witnessed at festivals.

Traditional Festivals in Time Perspective
"To live is to change", so writes Eric Moore (1976: 366). As dynamic events, African traditional festivals have continued over time, to undergo different kinds of change. In the homogeneous background of traditional African societies, change did take place in the manner people carried on their festivals. Contact among communities was limited and on small scale. People, however, learnt new dances, refurbished their masks,

and added new forms to their art and symbol collections. Change was natural and gradual in festivals in the traditional setting.

The trio of Commerce, Christianity and Colonialism from the 19th-century onwards, operated side by side in most parts of Africa, benefiting one another, more or less. It should be recalled that from its inception, shortly after the formal abolition of trans-Atlantic slave trade, the 19th-century project to introduce Christianity to different parts of sub-Saharan Africa, was visualised in terms of "a civilizing mission". Thomas Fowell Buxton's "African Civilisation Society" (ACS), formed in 1839 became a rallying forum for many British philanthropists, adventurers, merchants and evangelists (Gray 1980: 20). The sustained impact of those external socio-religious change-agents, and other forces associated with them including; western science, civilisation, modernity, urbanisation and industrialisation, have ever since engendered a radical kind of transformation in virtually every facet of life in Africa.

There have been systematic studies of socio-religious change in a number of individual African societies. A number of scholars highlight several stages in the radical transformation of the cultures and religious life of several African peoples. Felix Ekechi for example, breaks the duration of foreign impact and domination of Igbo society and culture into three stages. The first period stretches from the dawn of commerce and missionary Christianity to the establishment of colonial rule (1857-1900). The second stage spans some sixty years of intense missionary endeavour and the era of British domination (1900-1960). The third and final stage stretches from the dawn of independence to the present (1960- to-date). In respect of cultural and religious transformation, Ekechi characterizes the first stage as "the era of experimentation", the second as a period of "radical iconoclasm", and the third as the time of "cultural revival" (Ekechi 1977: 4).

Many Christian missionary groups waged sustained onslaught against aspects of traditional African cultures they viewed as either barbaric customs, or oppositionists cultural forms, including certain festivals. Such practices like the killing of twins by some communities, violent and destructive masquerades, certain initiation rites for young me and women, and cults were aggressively confronted. In some cases, colonial government administration gave their full backing to Christian missionary agents. In some others, the missionaries were alone in their opposition. In a related development, urbanisation, school education and prevailing economic realities have equally been taking their toll on festivals. Thousands of youths continue to leave rural areas to settle in cities. Many educated young people seem no longer keen to get initiated into age grade groups or masquerade societies. The consequence has been drastic for many traditional festivals in several parts of the Continent. Traditional people are forced to modify and adjust the form and manner several festivals are celebrated. Some festivals have simply become extinct.

Since independence, the trend towards cultural revival has been on the increase in several African countries. The development is of considerable benefit to several aspects of traditional cultures. Festivals, in particular, seem nowadays to be enjoying unprecedented attention from governments and its agencies, as well as cultural enthusiasts. The case of *Argungu* fishing festival of Argungu town in Kebbi State, Nigeria, is a classical example. The Federal Government of Nigeria has for sometime been participating actively in the celebration. This year's (2005) festival was graced by the physical presence of the President of Nigeria, Chief Olusegun Obasanjo. He pledged to encourage the celebration of the festival by committing large sums of money towards upgrading facilities at Argungu in order to bring them up to international standards.

The motive for the unprecedented current interest is no doubt, primarily economic as the need to boost tourism and attract much-needed foreign exchange and investment assumes greater prominence for many African countries. The recent attention can only augur well for traditional festivals. The development however, brings with it further changes in form and structure of many festivals. (It should be of interest to students of African cultures and researchers to investigate the impact of modern development on traditional African festivals). Masquerades, dance troupes, their costumes and other accoutrements for festivals are, on several occasions, moved about in buses and even aircrafts from one venue to another. It is also not uncommon these days to find artists, cultural troupes playing roles reserved to traditionally initiated persons. Several festivals are occasionally stage-managed purely for entertainment purposes. Aspects considered unsuitable or inappropriate for contemporary needs and situations, are simply eliminated.

Notwithstanding the current changes, communities in different parts of Africa continue to organise their festivals, often in adherence to their age-old ancestral traditions and for local consumption. But not infrequently these days, they are compelled by prevailing circumstances to respond also to external interests and needs in the way they celebrate.

Conclusion

Festivals are still an important aspect of contemporary African culture and life. They are found in their multiple variety in all parts of the Continent. They constitute an integral part of the total life-experience of different

African communities, including the ecological environments and socio-historical circumstances of people. They are multi-dimensional in character involving various facets of life, including the ecological, occupational and socio-historical circumstances. Their celebration is usually accompanied by stimulating dramatic scenes aimed, among other things, in providing useful distraction from the monotony of the ordinary routine of work and life.

Importantly, African traditional festivals are symbolic performance. They are sacred events often involving rich network of rituals. As symbols, they re-present multiple meanings at different levels of awareness at the same time. Festivals could at once relate to events of seasonal movement, and/or to the occupational and agricultural cycles as well as to important stages of the human life-cycle. They do equally encapsulate vital ideas and values concerning individual personality, as well as communal and mythical order.

The sacred character of traditional African festivals clearly signals their intricate connection with the indigenous world-view of the different peoples. In fact, the central issue which I have tried to elucidate in the paper is that the ultimate explanation and significance of festivals for traditional Africans lie within the cosmology of the different indigenous groups. Traditional festivals in Africa at once, involve human beings, as well as powerful spiritual figures. The activities of the latter are believed to be essentially interconnected with the general well-being and fortune of human beings and their world Festivals in traditional African background, ordinarily cater for the natural impulse and need which human beings have, occasionally to celebrate, relax and recreate. They equally mark significant transitions, episodes and landmarks in people's lives, their ecology, occupation, social environment, and history. All these aspects are fully integrated in festivals within the over-arching religious framework of traditional culture and life.

Note

*This essay is a revised version of a paper I published earlier in *Socio-Philosophical Perspective of African Traditional Religion*, edited by E. Ekpunobi and I. Ezeaku, (Enugu: New Age Publishers, 1990).

References

Anambra State Cultural Unit, *Traditional Festivals*, (Government Printers, Enugu, 1977).

Alagoa, E.J. and Tekena Tamuno (eds.), *Land and People of Nigeria: Rivers State*. Port Harcourt: Riverside Communications, 1989.

Callois, R. *Man and the Sacred*, translated by Meyer Barash. Glencoe: The Free Press, 1959.

Durkheim, E. *Elementary Forms of the Religious Life*. New York: The Free Press, 1965 (English trans.).

Eliade, M. *Cosmos and History, The Myth of Eternal Return*. New York: Harper and Row, 1959.

Horton, R. The Gods as Guests, *Nigerian Magazine*, Special Edition. Lagos: Government Printers, 1960.

Kalu, Ogbu, Precarious Vision, The Africa's Perception of His World, in Kalu, Ogbu (ed.) *African Cultural Development*. Enugu: Fourth Dimension Publishers, 1978.

Pieper, J. *Leisure, The Basis of Culture*, translated by Alexander Dru (New York; New American Library, Menter Book, 1963).

Pilgrim, R.B. Ritual in *Introduction to the Study of Religion*, T.M. Hall (ed.). New York: Harper and Row, 1978.

Opoku, A.A. *Festivals of Ghana*. Accra: Ghana Publishing Co., 1970).

8. The Innovations of John Wesley in Christendom and their Consequences for Africa

John H. Enemugwem
Department of History & Diplomatic Studies, University of Port Harcourt, Nigeria

This article grew out of the fact that the popular literatures on John Wesley omitted four of his contributions to Christendom and Africa. First are his endeavours to popularize the gospel in songs. Second is love offering. Third, he revived the ancient tradition of fasting that was moribund at the turn of the eighteenth century. Finally, the nonconformism of Wesley has serious implications for Africa. In an attempt to fill these gaps, this paper gives a critical assessment of the innovations of Wesley. The aspect of its implications for the black continent seems plausible since historical sense involves a perception of not only the remoteness of the events, but also for its consequences in later years.[1] Putting these appraisals in one document will improve our understanding of John Wesley and his times.

Introduction

John Wesley and his followers belong to the Christian religion.[2] Christianity is one of the four principal religions in the world. Others are Islam, Judaism and the traditional religions. Unlike these three, Christianity began as a sectarian group within Judaism and was inaugurated by the apostles of Jesus Christ before Saint Paul expanded it to Rome and transformed it into a world religion in the first century A.D.[3] The Christian religion uses the lifestyles, teachings, death and resurrection of Jesus Christ as the tenet of its doctrine. These are published as the *New Testament* by his early followers. Together with the oral traditions of the Jews known as the *Old Testament*, both works constitute the *Holy Bible* used by Christians, including John Wesley and his group, in worshipping God.

Of course, long before the birth of John Wesley, Christianity had been characterised by three principal sects, the Roman Catholic Church, the Eastern Orthodox Church and the Protestants. The Protestants later split into many denominations. This created room for Wesley's Methodist Church to emerge from the Anglican Communion with innovations and implications for Africa. First in our assessment are the early years of Wesley.

Early Years
John Wesley was born on 17 June, 1703 at Epworth in Lincolnshire, England, to the Reverend Samuel Wesley (1662-1735) and Mrs. Susannah Wesley (1669 – 1742)[4]. He was their fifteenth child and second surviving son of

their nineteenth children. At this time, his father was the Rector of the Anglican Parish, Epworth, from 1695 – 1735, and a well connected clergy of the Church of England. Prior to Epworth, the Reverend Samuel was the Vicar of South Ormsby, also in Lincolnshire, from his ordination in 1690 to 1695. He married John's mother when the latter was nineteen years of age. Ecclesiastical history stated how she was spending sixty minutes every morning and evening in prayer and meditation.[5] Although she is said to have started it before marrying John's father, the nineteen children they had within the first twenty one years of their wedlock could not disturb her meditation culture. Ten that survived them, six girls and four boys, received her splendid care and affection that enkindled their growth to move England forward. Hence, Samuel and Susannah had no regret for the death of their nine children at infancy.

Under these conditions, John and his brothers and sisters could not form their own habits but take after their parents. None of them above the age of one was allowed to cry aloud in their home nor eat between meals and have a choice of food other than what their parents provide. They were also not allowed for games on Sunday. As they were always punished for disobedience unless they voluntarily confess their guilt, they were also rewarded for obedience. It is on record that John's mother was going apart awhile every day with each of her children for meditation and counselling. John's day was Thursday.⁶ After his mother's demise, he kept to it as his sacred day because he started with her at his birth.

Nevertheless, the period of John's birth is important in European history. He was born at the eve of a new world order when Europe was laying the foundation of modernization, industrialization and nationalism. Secondly, the year preceding his birth witnessed the crowning of the last reigning Stuart, Queen Anne. Before her reign terminated in 1714, England had united with Scotland in 1707 and became known as Great Britain or United Kingdom.⁷ Indeed, the union of these two nations is viewed by historians as the greatest achievement of the Stuarts which took place in the year John's younger brother, Charles Wesley, was born on December 18 as the eighteenth child of his parents.⁸

In 1709, John was six years young when their house was burnt and they narrowly escaped death. He refused to browse over their sorrows but turned the situation into an incentive to render voluntary services to God and man. His parents also moved beyond self-pity, drew inspiration from the event and encouraged their children for the service of God.

Diligence led the Reverend Samuel Wesley into serious thinking on where to send John and Charles for a sound education. He gave considerable regard to Oxford University where he trained at Exeter College in 1683, before their births. As a result, John was educated at the famous Charterhouse School London, from 1714 to 1720, and Christ Church Oxford, where he obtained his B.A and M.A. (Theology) in 1724 and 1727. Charles too had his own at Westminster School where he was the King's scholar and captain of the school. He also attended Christ Church, Oxford, excelled distinctively, and was appointed a college tutor.[9]

Obviously, another clue to John's early life came from his activities at Oxford. During their years at Christ Church, Charles Wesley formed the Holy Club to promote Christian ethics and social services to the poor. As soon as John Wesley joined the club on his return to Oxford as a graduate student, he was made the leader. His leadership role imposed intensive Bible study, prayer and fasting on the group. It was not only an exemplary record that he was setting but also a methodological approach to the Christian religion. Before John finished his studies in 1727 and became Fellow of Lincoln College Oxford, he was known throughout the United Kingdom as the leader of the band of "Oxford Methodists".[10]

These virtues led John Wesley into the ordinate ambition and he received the Holy Orders in the Church of England. In fact, from his deaconate in 1725 to his priesthood in 1728, he had his curacy with his father at Epworth. The brief period of it exposed his ecclesiastical acumen in celebrating the Eucharist, preaching the gospel and in musical rendition. He combined these with his academic appointment at Oxford as Lecturer in Greek (New Testament) until his mission to the United States of America in 1735.

It should, however, be mentioned that the year 1735 remained unique in Wesley's life. This was the time he went to Georgia, USA, as a missionary of the Society for the Propagation of the Gospel of Jesus Christ in New England. His mission was to Christianize the American Indians and bring them into Western civilization. Founded in 1649 by the Church of England to support missionary work in the New World, the Society first used the Reverend John Eliot to achieve her aim.[11] Eliot worked in Massachusetts in the American Indian community called Waban. He was able to rehabilitate and convert them to Christianity. He also established 14 small towns and churches for them, translated the *Holy Bible* from English to the American Indian vernacular. It was the first Bible to be printed in America.[12] In addition to training teachers and ministers, Eliot founded the Indian College at Cambridge and the Free School in Roxbury, both in Massachusetts, before his expiration in the 1680s. But John Wesley could only leave for America after his father's death at Epworth on 25 April, 1735. Charles accompanied him in the same year as a member of the Georgia Mission and as Secretary to General James

Edward Oglethorpe, the Governor of Georgia. This was after his ordination in the Church of England in 1735.

In Farah's findings, the result of their mission was unfruitful.[13] They could neither convert the Georgia Indians to Christianity nor reform them. Charles quickly noticed it and returned home in 1736 after spending five months. But John lingered on for three years. However, specific reasons accounted for Wesley's ineffectiveness in America. Instead of facing his missionary work he diverted his attention to fighting the Atlantic Slave Trade, the immoral acts of the slavers and his colleague clergymen who were in support of it.[14] At last, he returned home without fulfilling his mission to America.

On arrival in England on February 1, 1738, John felt he was a failure. His lack of courage nearly drove him to commit suicide. But he later learnt the attributes of courage from a Moravian missionary, Peter Böhler, who was a follower of Count von Zinzendorf. He took John to their centre in Germany and told him that the only thing he needed was faith.[15] From here he went through the activities which led to the founding of Methodist Church and the inauguration of open air preaching in Christendom.

The Founding of Methodist Church & Open Air Preaching

John Wesley pioneered these two frontiers that added colour to the Christian religion. Exactly on 24 May 1738, the first activity which generated them took place. On that day he reluctantly attended a fellowship meeting organized by his friend, Peter Böhler, in a Moravian Chapel at Aldergate Street, London. When a layman recited St. Paul's letter to the Ephesians, John Wesley immediately experienced a strange but strong enthusiasm for God which indicated the forgiveness of his sins.[16] Thereafter, he started preaching salvation by faith to unprecedented audiences. His sole aim was to bring back true Christianity that was almost eluding England. At this period, morals were rotten and Christianity was decaying. Honour and credit worthiness were the key words of Wesley's religious intercourse. Being the cornerstone of a sound religious reputation, these qualities made him exceptional in the Anglican Communion after his conversion.

However, some grievances drove the Anglican authorities to close their pulpit against Wesley. First, he was the target of public opinion against his itinerant preaching in the morning when people were still in bed. This forced the English lords to call his religious enthusiasm "superstitious nonsense".[17] Second, the English Crown rarely liked how Wesley lowered religion to the capacity of the down trodden who were his major crowd. Most of them were coming from far to listen to his criticisms of the immorality and hypocrisy in the Church of England. The sights of his audience were reminding the British powers that leaving John Wesley in the English Church could cause an unwanted revolution. As a result, when he preached in June 1738 at a public square in London, his opponents brought an ox to disperse his crowd of about 20,000 people. But a surprising thing happened. The ox that was obedient to the owners became disobedient and refused their bidding. In the second command, it faced its handlers, ran through them and there was a great panic but without touching John Wesley's audience.[18]

Another predominant reason for his excommunication was how Wesley's audience often reacted emotionally by screaming, shouting, crying penitently and fainting to a near death point after hearing his provocative sermons. From all indications, the social temper in the Church of England was rather high. They saw him as a rebel. Owing to these facts, he and his brother, Charles Wesley (1707-1788) who had his evangelical awakening on a Whitsunday three days before him, were excommunicated.[19]

These two brothers, now ecclesiastical leaders without denominations, were unprepared to return to the English Church. They were to preach the gospel wherever people gathered. This became evident as they went into open-air preaching, using fields, street corners, large outdoor spaces, private homes, and motor parks. They also travelled extensively on horsebacks delivering their charismatic sermons that sent listeners into immediate conversions. The nature and development of these approaches to Christianity identified them and their numerous converts as the Methodists.

According to Udensi, at the close of 1738, they had built a church without naming it after any denomination.[20] Their first watch night service was held in this new church on 31 December, 1738. At midnight when worshippers were leaving to welcome the New Year Day, John Wesley remained behind praying for the reformation of Britain from moral decadence. It is significant to note that as soon as Charles Wesley did not see his brother, John, in the crowd surging out of their new church, he went back looking for him and met him praying. He called others back to tarry with John till dawn. Nevertheless, the power of God is said to have descended on them at 3.00 a.m. of the New Year Day, 1739 and many of them cried out of joy and fell on the ground, singing *Tedeum Laudamus*. They viewed this event, which inspired their evangelism, as their "Pentecost". Other frontline participants in the watch night service were Messrs Hall, Kinchin, Ingham, Whitefield, Hutchins, Williams, Charles Wesley and members of the Holy Club.[21] They also celebrated the Love Feast with John Wesley at Fetherland on the same January 1, 1739 before travelling to different destinations to spread their new concept of "salvation by faith and scriptural holiness".

In the light of their new dispensation, Wesley was elated at the first anniversary of their conversion. This reason made Charles to compose a hymn on 21 May, 1739, "O for a Thousand Tongues to Sing", in praise of their great Redeemer. According to European and African sources, the title emanates from Peter Böhler's remark at Wesley's conversion in May, 1738 thus, "Had I a thousand tongues I would praise Him with them all".[22] Historical interpretation has it that Wesley's publication of this song in their *Hymns and Sacred Poems* (1740) and its update as the first hymn in *The Methodist Hymn Book* (1933) was to enable Christians fulfil their wish of thanking God unceasingly.

It must not be forgotten that the progress of John Wesley's fervent evangelism was noticed far and near. A case in point is his engagement for Sunday 20 May, 1759, at Everton, England.[23] Before his arrival, the large building used as the venue of his crusade was filled with 32,000 persons, both inside and outside. To Wesley "people seemed almost stifled by their breath".[24] Some of them came on foot from places of 13 miles and above, starting their journey at 2.00 am. Rather than the crusade solving their problems only, it made them followers of Wesley and propagators of the gospel of Jesus Christ.

John Wesley established two things through which the Methodist Communion was inaugurated. First, his 40,000 sermons[25] to large audiences enabled him to raise 175,000 persons as the Methodists.[26] Second, after much persuasion, Wesley organized these followers into Methodist societies and chapels governed by a Central Methodist Conference led by him. He also ordained over 600 lay preachers for the chapels. While the conference supervised the lay preachers and their chapels, the latter were to assist themselves in good works and preaching the gospel. In fact, among the first ordained preachers by John Wesley were Dr. Thomas Coke and Francis Asbury. They organized the American Methodist ministry.[27] After his death in March 1791, they became an independent Christian denomination.[28] This caused a schism within the Church of England which was the fears of the English lords. However, ministering the gospel in songs commands a major part of the Methodist Church liturgy.

Ministering the Gospel in Songs

John Wesley in his life-time developed a flair for good music and the gospel. Like his father and brother, Charles, he combined these two things and never broke an appointment to perform them, no matter the distance. Because he was a singer of sermons and publisher of the

Christian religious music, people were always eager to hear him singing from memory as well as knowing the new compositions. Hence his engagement venues were always thronged by listeners.

However, there is evidence that John and Charles Wesley popularized the ministration of the gospel in songs.[29] As at 1738 when they were excommunicated from the Anglican Communion and became singing evangelists, no Christian denomination had greater variety of hymns than the Methodists. One factor that aided them was John's translation of songs from the German, French and Spanish hymn books into English. Their progression to original composition of hymns came as a result of dearth of hymn books in the English speaking world. For this reason, in 1753 John Wesley published *Hymns and Spiritual Songs* that eased congregational singing in the United Kingdom. Prior to this date, he had published several gospel song books in major European languages at a reduced price of one shilling.[30]

John Wesley's first work, *Collection of Psalms and Hymns*, was published in 1737 at Savannah, Georgia in U.S.A. This was when he discovered lack of hymn books in the Americas. Other works by him include *Wesley's Hymns and Sacred Poems* (1740), *Morning Hymn Book* (1741), *A Collection of Tunes Set to Music as they are Commonly Sung at Foundery* (1742), *Hymns for the Nativity of Our Lord* (1744), *Hymns for Our Lord's Resurrection* (1746), *The Wesleyan Funeral Hymns* (1759), *Select Hymns with Tunes Annext* (1765), *Sacred Melody* (1780), *The Wesleyan Hymn Book* (1780), *The Large Hymn Book* (1780) and *Collection of Hymns* (1780). He also contributed to the following works of Charles Wesley, *Hymns for Times of Trouble and Persecution* (1744), *Hymns for those that Seek and those that have Redemption in the Blood of Christ* (1747), *Hymns of Intercession for all Mankind* (1758), *Short Hymns on Select Passages of the Holy Scripture* (1762), among others.[31]

Wesley was using these sacred songs to minister the gospel to large congregations. A Methodist clergy[32] once told this author that Wesley used his family hymn, "Forth in Thy Name, O Lord I Go" (1740) to preach godliness to the crowd of 32, 000 persons at Everton in May 1759. So also are "Soldiers of Christ Arise", whose wordings were taken from Ephesians 6:10-17, and "Love Divine, all Loves Excelling". In these and various other ways, it did not take the world time to realise the inclination of the Wesley family to music. Being great hymn writers and translators, they rendered the greatest service to religion through music. The world knows their significance in the encouragement they gave Christians in congregational singing and no hymnal of most denominations could do without their compositions.

In the history of church music, Charles Wesley alone composed 6,500 hymns.[33] One of it, "Jesus Lover of My Soul", first published in *Wesleyans Hymns and Sacred Poems* (1740) has an interesting story behind it. Oral and written sources stated that one morning children played in Charles Wesley's churchyard and pursued a hawk that flew into his vicarage for safety.[34] While he protected the bird from death, the solitude it underwent for a whole day led him to compose this popular song. Being a poet, the composition was brisk and Charles Wesley kept singing it until the bird that took solace in his bosom flew away safely.

This composer put his best endeavours in making the Methodist a singing people. It could be recalled that he left 2,800 hymns in manuscript at his death on 29 March, 1788.[35] While his hymns peculiarly fitted every occasion, it rent the air at his burial in the St. Marylebone's Churchyard, London. Like their great forebears, the generations of Wesley never relent in ministering the gospel in songs. Charles Wesley's children namely, Charles Wesley (Jr.) (1757-1834) and Samuel Wesley (1766-1837) are examples. Charles (Jr.) composed the hymn tune, "Epworth", in remembrance of the birthplace of his father and uncle John, and was responsible for the revision and publication of the songbook, *Sacred Harmony*, in 1821.[36] As for Samuel, he was a great composer, first class violinist and the most masterly organist of his time whose works transcend the Protestant to the Roman Catholic Communions. He conducted the great Birmingham Festival in 1811 and was renowned before the age of eight when he put the biblical book of Ruth into an oratorio.[37]

It is not unfair to mention another musical landmark in the Wesley family. Thus, Samuel Wesley in the course of good music named his son, Samuel Sebastian Wesley (1810-1876), after himself and his musical idol, Sebastian Bach, and trained him to doctorate degree in music. At the age of 16, Samuel Sebastian was a reputable organist. In his later years, he published *The European Psalmist* (1872) of 733 hymn tunes and rendered one of the finest services in English Church music. His greatness was unfolded before he became the Gloucester Cathedral organist where he conducted the Three Choirs Festival that made Britain proud of his citizenship.[38]

Earlier before them, John Wesley (1703 – 1791) had described human heritage of good music as what can promote one's relationship with God. His love for music did not end with the Wesleyan compositions like his junior brother, Charles Wesley (1707 – 1788). Other hymn writers like Isaac Watts (1674 – 1748) benefited from John Wesley's expertise in publishing Church music. Hence, both of them were joint authors of hymns.[39] In fact, John Wesley's best song was Isaac Watts' hymn, "I'll Praise My Maker while I've Breath", which he continued singing until he closed his eyes in death on March 2, 1791 in London.[40] Fortunately, his introduction of "love offering" and the revival of "weekly fasting" contributed to the effectiveness of the Christian religion.

Wesley and the Advent of Love Offering and Revival of Fasting

John Wesley took critical steps in introducing love offering and the revival of Wednesday and Friday fasting which contributed to the tenets of his evangelical revival. This fact signifies that in the early 1700s when there was no love offering in the Church of England, tithing held sway. Thus, tithing means a tenth of one's income to the church for the service of God. During the period of Wesley, the inadequacy of the English Church to satisfy its aspirations and eradicate its financial straits was widely noticed. As a result, he introduced love offering by putting 50% of his earnings into the Church and viewed it as what could allow Christians to give as their minds detect.[41]

Of course, it is also commonly accepted that the revival of the Wednesday and Friday fasting, presently observed in the Christian religion, came from the critical role of John Wesley. Records proved that it was moribund before his period due to some Londoners that fasted excessively and impaired their health.[42] The relative importance of this ancient practice of Christian self denial dawned on Wesley during his educational career at Charterhouse, London, and Christ Church, Oxford. There, he made it a rule for every member of the Holy Club and his close associates to fast on these two days in the week, except prevented by ill health. Fasting has been a strong topic of our hero's evangelism for over half a century. In his evangelical revival of Ireland in 1789, he told the world that "the man that never fasts is no more in the way to Heaven than the man that never prays".[43] He linked the causes of inefficacy of Christianity to the abandonment of fasting by Christians. To forestall it, he advocated for the 6.00am – 3.00pm fasting on Wednesday and Friday.

On the whole, John Wesley succeeded in harmonizing the Christian world with his evangelism. In Europe, the Americas and Australia, Wesley's appeal went mostly to the underprivileged and increased their sobriety, diligence, self-effacing and self-discipline. It is remarkable that his evangelism instilled peace and sanitized England. At this point, Industrial Revolution was realised in 1760.[44] Hence, his joy became unhidden when he vociferated, "I will not snatch a child from the devil without nurturing him".[45] He was more of a latitudinarian in his religious dogma which altered the history of England. But then the full strategic consequences of his reformation seem to fall on Africa.

Consequences for Africa

The importance of John Wesley is highly noticed in the black continent where his works endured in the social, economic and political histories. It is necessary to detail the arguments on which it is based. First, is the social aspect of eradicating slavery and slave trade.

The Abolition of Slavery and Slave Trade

This social impact of Wesley's work started in 1735 during his mission to America. There he saw slavery as morally dehumanizing and an inhuman practice that needs abolition. In point of fact, the degeneration of the slaves and Wesley's encounter with the illicit trade in human cargo fired his zeal to advocate for three things. He called for the emancipation and evangelization of the slaves as well as the abolition of slave trade and slavery. However, the slavers disagreed on three principles. They argued that slavery is a social matter while slave trade is an economic activity. Thirdly, they implored Wesley to channel his evangelical energy towards the American Indians. But our protagonist of anti-slavery rather took both slavers and the slaves as sinners for conversion.[46]

One of the things the Church of England used in excommunicating our hero was his first attack on them. Thus, while in the United States, he accused the English Church of supporting slavery and slave trade. According to Fage, the Anglican Communion in the eighteenth century was committed to the protection of properties and their owners including slaves and slavers.⁴⁷ As a result, some Christian missionaries in Africa participated in slave trading just as any other trader.⁴⁸

The slave situation was such that Wesley directed the weight of his evangelism towards the formation of the Anti-Slavery Movement. This materialized fully in 1765 when legislators like Henry Thorton and William Wilberforce, Cambridge graduates like Thomas and John Clarkson as well as Granville Sharp, responded to his call. Using Wesley's evangelical connection, the campaign was heightened in Europe, the Americas and Africa. Between 1772 and 1872 slavery and slave trade were abolished. According to Inikori, "during the whole period of the slave trade, about 25 million people, at least, were sent out of Africa, South of the Sahara".⁴⁹ All in all, John Wesley's failure to reform the American Indians saved Africa from slave trade and slavery and brought the inauguration of Western political models in West Africa.

Introduction of Western Political Models in West Africa

Measured by this yardstick, the spill over effect of the social impact created the political consequences for Africa, beginning in 1787. Take, for example, the freedom given to slaves in Lord Mansfield's judgement in 1772 left 15,000 slaves emancipated in England and in 1785 the number had risen to 30,000. Almost all of them and the 1,200 from Nova Scotia that fought for Britain in the 1783 War of American Independence were used in establishing the Colony of Sierra Leone in 1787.[50] Prior to John Wesley's death in 1791, the Sierra Leone Company was incorporated and commissioned by Act of Parliament to administer the new Colony. The Governors of Sierra Leone were responsible for the protection of British affairs all over West Africa. From here the European political model was introduced in the sub-region. This inspiration later drove the American Colonization Society to establish the Republic of Liberia in 1822 for the American freed slaves.[51]

Before the period under review, Britain had never wanted to establish colonies again. This was due to their loss of America in the 1783 War of Independence. What changed her mind was the evangelical pressure of John Wesley. It is on record that his follower and pioneer Methodist minister, Dr. Thomas Coke, was the first European in 1787 to plan for the establishment of missions, abroad.[52] His efforts led to the founding of the British Missionary Society in 1792, the Church Missionary Society in 1799, the British and Foreign Bible Society in 1804 and the Wesleyan Missionary Society in 1813. The values placed on Africa by these missions to

Christianize, Commercialize and Colonize, was a wisdom Britain could not disapprove.

However, the Methodist of John Wesley implemented the doctrine of these trinitarian Cs and opened up Nigeria for Britain. On 24 September, 1842, the Reverend Thomas Birch Freeman of the Wesleyan Mission came to Nigeria and stationed at Badagry. Being the pioneer missionary to the country in the nineteenth century, he discovered that Britain was only after the palm produce trade in the Eastern Niger Delta and not the abolition of slave trade and colonization. Hence in early 1843 he appealed to Captain L. T. Jones of the Preventive Squadron to commence the anti-slave trade treaty from Niger Delta to Badagry.[53] He argued that it was in accordance with John Wesley's anti-slavery scheme. Except it is first done in the Delta and Yorubaland the slave trade that was going on will not give way for the palm produce trade. This was urgently fulfilled.

Another thing of crucial significance in the Wesleyan work in Nigeria is Freeman's appeal to Governor George Maclean of the Gold Coast. He wanted Maclean to include Nigeria in his British Protectorate.[54] In response, Maclean transferred Sergeant Bart, a Fante soldier, of the Gold Coast Corps to Nigeria in August 1843. As soon as this was accomplished, the Methodist Mission House Badagry, built by Freeman, became the seat of government. It is interesting to note that Bart hoisted the first British flag, the Union Jack, in Nigeria and offered British protection to the people. With the Cape Coast Castle of Governor Maclean backing him, his fiat was law.

By the end of 1844 Sergeant Bart was withdrawn. Britain substituted his services with that of John Beecroft (1790-1854) whose consular administration was much felt in the Niger Delta and Badagry.[55] After him in 1853, several British officials ruled Nigeria until her independence in 1960. From this small beginning, not only British empire building was realised in West Africa but also a revolution in the economy, education and architecture.

A Revolution in the Nigerian Economy, Education and Architecture

Further explanation could also be offered in the area of economic consequence of John Wesley's innovations. As soon as Nigeria became a part of the British Protectorate of Governor Maclean in 1843, Badagry became a commercial centre where British vessels transacted business.[56] As this was happening the Reverend Freeman and his assistant Wesleyan missionaries, Mr & Mrs. William de Graft, were putting the people through in modern agriculture. They introduced pineapple, guinea corn, apples, guava and cocoa farming in the country.[57] Cocoa farming, from then onward, became the economy of the Yoruba, Boki and Idoma peoples of Nigeria.

The third factor was Freeman's establishment of European architecture in Nigeria. This started with the building of Methodist Mission House at Badagry. By the time the Methodist Church was established at several places in the country, Africans were engaged in the construction of the buildings. They were trained in various skills including building construction, carpentry and joinery, sawing, masonry, brick and tile making, draughtsmanship and town planning. Suffice it to say that this Methodist Mission House at Badagry shown below, which gulped £300 is the pioneer storey building in Nigeria.[58]

Another merit of the Wesleyans was their introduction of Western education in Nigeria. Thus, the first known primary school in this country was established in 1843 by Mr & Mrs. William de Graft. According to Fafunwa, the school which was christened "Nursery of the Infant Church" was started at Badagry with 40 pupils as a method of evangelization.[59] It was from here that Western education spread all over Nigeria and its products revolutionized the Nigerian economy as well as the political and social well-being of the people. Hence the Methodist is a reference point in the history of Western education in Nigeria.

The first storey building in Nigeria at Badagry

Authenticating these facts is the special emphasis of a former British Consul in the Niger Delta, Harry H. Johnston. According to him, the white man could not have been Governor in Africa, exploiter and teacher without the work of the missionaries. The latter were responsible for the inauguration and maintenance of the protectorates and colonies as well as evangelical revival in the African Church[60].

Evangelical Revival in the African Church
Mbiti recalled that Christianity took root early in Africa and grew into an indigenous religion in North Africa, the Horn and the Mediterranean.[61] Its fruits were some of the early martyrs and contributors to Christendom. One of the contributors, Saint Augustine of Hippo (AD 354-430),

was not only an eminent scholar and Bishop in the Roman Catholic Church but also a member of the Christian Council. He defended the Christian faith, developed the Christian traditions and calendar, established more monasteries for the training of monks and used his work, *The City of God,* among others, to revolutionize historiography.[62] Except in Ethiopia, the Islamic times of AD 600-1800 had reduced the influence of Christianity in the continent.

However, evangelical revival was actually experienced from the nineteenth century when European Christian missions came to West Africa. As a result, the pioneer Christian denomination established in the most populated African nation, Nigeria, in 1842 was the Methodist Church of John Wesley which spread to everywhere. In the findings of Olali, it preceded other denominations in the Gambia, Sierra Leone, Republic of Benin and Ghana, among other places.[63] Hence, similar measures of Wesley's evangelism greeted the Nigerian Church between 1881 and 1920 and the Beninese Church in 1947, to mention few instances.

The records make it clear that the evangelical renewal in Nigeria was prompted by the peoples' thirst for African culture and Wesley's innovations. Thus, in 1881 some Anglican communicants in Lagos, led by Dr. Edward Wilmot Blyden, agitated for the inclusion of these into the liturgy to enable them evangelize the hinterland. They envisaged for the ministration of the gospel in African songs, clapping of hands, drumming and dancing to its rhythm, love offering and excessive prayer and fasting. Unexpectedly, the opposition of the European missionaries drove them to form the United Native African Church in 1891 and the African Church in 1901 with polygamy in their doctrine.[64]

The popularity of their Africanness in worshipping God went far and near and became the springboard of many indigenous religious organizations. One of it was the Precious Stone Society founded in 1920 by a goldsmith, Joseph Shadare and a teacher, Miss Sophia Odulami. They pleaded with their parent denomination, St. Saviour's (Anglican) Church Ijebu-Ode in 1918, to accept open air crusade and African music into the liturgy. Rather than attending to these demands, they excommunicated them. But people benefited from the healing campaigns of this new Church through prayer and fasting.[65]

In the Niger Delta, too, there was a far-reaching revival. Tasie stresses the nonconformism of a Kalabari canoe-carver and trader, Garrick Idaketima Sokari Braide.[66] Born at Bakana Town in the 1800s, he was an Anglican communicant, licensed lay preacher, pastor's warden and a Board member of the Niger Delta Pastorate. After the Reverend M.A. Kemmer had inducted him into true Christianity, he toed the line of

John Wesley and was going apart awhile for excessive prayer and fasting, praying for seventeen times a day.[67] Consequently, Garrick developed a divine power and converted thousands into the Christian religion. They had thronged his open air crusades of faith healing sermons and destroyed all their non-Christian deities. At the turn of 1916, his movement had over a million converts for the Niger Delta Pastorate. According to Ayandele, "Garrick Braide achieved in three month what the Church Missionary Society had not attained in half a century".[68] Being a spiritual healer of all ailments without cost, he introduced love offering in the Niger Delta Church.

A much more important factor in determining his evangelical revival came to light in 1908. Oral evidence from two members of his family recollected the day a social club in Bakana was having a festive occasion.[69] They assembled some Igbo native doctors to prevent rain from falling. But Garrick debated with them that he can pray God to flood Bakana with heavy rainfall. He did not end his prayers when everywhere was flooded with an unprecedented rain. In his views, this came by prayer and fasting. He was, therefore, likened to the Biblical Prophet Elijah and from henceforth became known as Prophet Elijah II in the Niger Delta and beyond.

Like John Wesley, never did Garrick intend to cause schism anywhere. But it came when the Delta Church, headed by Bishop James Johnson, and the British colonial administration of Nigeria excommunicated and imprisoned him in 1916. The reasons were the popularity of his movement which reduced the population of this Church by nine-tenth and denied the colonial government an annual revenue of £576,000 due to the abstinence of his adherents from alcohol.[70] After his death in the prison on Friday 15 November, 1918, his million devotees from the Niger Delta and its hinterland turned his movement into Christ Army Church.

Nevertheless, local preference of African culture and Wesley's innovations were also there in the Beninese Church.[71] Being the reason that brought out Samuel Bilewu Joseph Oshoffa from the Methodist Church, Porto Novo, Republic of Benin, he founded the Celestial Church of Christ on Monday 29September, 1947.There are more of these innovative Christian denominations in Africa. Their branches all over the continent propagate evangelical renewal which John Wesley instigated in Christendom.

Conclusion

This work assesses the role of John Wesley in Christendom and how it affected Africa. He was born in 1703 and trained at the Charterhouse School, London, and Christ Church, Oxford. After taking the Holy Orders in the Church of England, he served his father as a curate at Epworth and taught Theology at Oxford before leaving for America in 1735. His unfruitful mission to Christianize the Georgian Indians in U.S.A gave him the leeway to embark on other Christian activities. This led to the founding of the Methodist Church and open air preaching in Christendom. Through this means, he and his brother, Charles, popularized the ministration of the gospel in songs. But then his introduction of love offering and revival of the weekly fasting furthered the course of Christianity.

The serious implications for Africa could be found in the social, political and economic spheres. The Anti-Slavery Movement founded by John Wesley paved the way for the abolition of slavery and slave trade, the founding of the Colony of Sierra-Leone and the Republic of Liberia to accommodate the freed slaves. As a result, the European political system was planted in West Africa. In the same vein, the Wesleyan missionaries that pioneered British imperialism in Nigeria also introduced the Western educational system, European architecture and modern agriculture. These innovations that revolutionized the African economy, political and social organizations drew strength from the teachings of John Wesley (1703-1791).

Notes and References

1. T.S. Eliot cited in M. Farah, et al., *The Human Experience* (Columbus, Ohio: Merrill Publishing House, 1985) p. iii.
2. *The New Encyclopaedia Britannica*, 15th ed. Vol. 3 (Chicago: Encyclopedia Britannica, 1998) p.280.
3. *Ibid*.
4. Luke Tyerman, *The Life and Times of the Reverend Samuel Wesley* (London: The Author, 1973) passim.
5. "Saints of Old", *Life: The Magazine for the Victorious Life*, No. 6 (Lagos: Deeper Christian Life Ministry, 2004) p. 5.
6. *Ibid*.
7. T.W. Wallbank, *et al. History and Life: The World and Its People*, 3rd ed. (Glenview, Illinois: Scott, Foresman, 1987) p.447.
8. A.C. Outler, "Charles Wesley", in *The Encyclopedia Americana: International Edition*, Vol. 28 (Connecticut: Grolier, 1995) p.630.
9. M. Farah, et al., *The Human Experience* (Columbus, Ohio: Merrill, 1985) p. 340.
10. Adam Clarke, *Memoirs of the Wesley Family* (London: The Author, 1823) passim.
11. R.J. Jay, *Christians You Should Know* (Benin City: Joint Heirs, n.d) pp 7-13.
12. *Ibid*. p.12.

13. Farah, *The Human Experience*, p. 340.
14. "Thoughts on Slavery", in *The Works of the Reverend John Wesley* Vol. XI (London, 1872) pp. 64-65.
15. R.G. Turtle Jr., *John Wesley: His Life and Theology* (Zondervan: The Author, 1982) passim.
16. G.C. Cell, *The Rediscovery of John Wesley* (Amsterdam: University Press, 1983).
17. A.C. Outler (ed.) *The Works of John Wesley* (Amsterdam: University Press, 1984) passim.
18. "Saints of Old", in *Life Magazine*, No. 6, August 2004. p 4.
19. W.J. Duiker and J. J. Spielvogel, *World History*, 2nd ed. (Belmont: Wadsworth, 1998) pp.675-676.
20. J.K. Udensi, *Methodist Revival and Evangelism: Past, Present and Future*, (Aba: Faith Clinic, 2001) pp. 8, 11.
21. *Ibid.*
22. J.M. Barkley (ed.) *Handbook to the Church Hymnary*, 3rd ed. (London: O.U.P, 1979)p. 153; F.N. Akah and D.L. Emmanuel, *Understanding Hymnody: Traditions of Christian Hymns and Canticles*, Vol. 1 (Port Harcourt: Link Advertising, 2002) pp37-39.
23. E.H. Sugden and Joseph Allison (eds.) *Wesley's Standard Sermons* (Zondervan Press, 1986).
24. John Wesley, cited in Duiker and Spielvogel, *World History*, pp.675-676.
25. James Miller, "God has Told Us in His Word", *Herald of His Coming* Vol.31 No.11 (Nov. 1972) pp. 6-7.

26. Farah, *The Human Experience* p.340.
27. H.P. Slatte, *Fire in the Brand: An Introduction to the Creative Works and Theology of John Wesley* (Amsterdam: University Press, 1983) passim.
28. *The Journal of John Wesley* (Zondervan Press, 1986) passim.
29. *The Methodist Hymn Book with Tune* (London: Methodist Conference Office, 1933) pp. iii, v.
30. John Wesley, "Preface to a Collection of Hymns for Use of the People called Methodists", *The Methodist Hymn Book with Tunes*, p. v.
31. *The Methodist Hymn Book with Tunes*, pp. ii-xi, Cf. Barkley (ed.) *Handbook to the Church Hymnary*, passim.
32. The Reverend Ezekiel Pepple of the Methodist Church Nigeria in a personal communication, June, 1980.
33. Barkley (ed.) *Handbook to the Church Hymnary*, p. 368.
34. Oral account of the Reverend Ezekiel Pepple in June 1980. Cf. Akah and Emmanuel, *Understanding Hymnody*, p.135.
35. Outler, "Charles Wesley", in *The Encyclopedia Americana*, p. 630.
36. *The Methodist Hymn Book with Tunes*, pp.xi, 325& 1019.
37. Barkley, *The Handbook to the Church Hymnary* p. 369.
38. *Ibid.* pp.369-370. Cf. *The Methodist Hymn Book with Tunes*, p. xi.
39. *The Church Hymnary*, 3rd ed. (Oxford: O.U.P., 1973) pp.4, 555, 581.

40. *The Methodist Hymn Book with Tunes*, p. iv. Cf. R. L. Moore, *John Wesley and Authority* (London: Scholars Press, 1979).
41. Personal communications with the Reverend Jacob Dickson of the Anglican Communion, Nigeria, May 1994.
42. Miller, "God has Told Us in His Word", pp. 6-7.
43. John Wesley, "The Causes of Inefficacy of Christianity: A Sermon Delivered in Ireland in 1789", cited in *Herald of His Coming,* Vol. 31 No. 11 (Nov. 1972) pp. 6-7.
44. T.S. Ashton, *The Industrial Revolution, 1760-1830*, (Oxford: O.U.P., 1968) pp.14-17.
45. Udensi, *Methodist Revival and Evangelism*, p.11.
46. *The Works of The Reverend John Wesley*, Vol. xi (London, 1872) pp 64-65.
47. J.D. Fage, *A History of West Africa* (Cambridge: C.U.P, 1969) pp. 111-112, 118-121.
48. O.U. Kalu, "Gathering Figs and Thistles?: Slavery and Christianization of Igboland", *Nigerian Heritage,* Vol.8 (1999)p.12; Cf. W. H. Mobley, *The Ghanaian's Image of the Missionary*, (Leiden: E. J. Brill, 1972) passim.
49. J.E. Inikori, "The Origin of the Diaspora: The Slave Trade from Africa", *Tarikh,* Vol.5 No. 4 (1978) p.14.
50. M.B. Akpan, "The Return to Africa: Sierra Leone and Liberia" *Tarikh,* Vol.5 No.4 (1978) pp. 92-116, 120-121.

51. J.B. Webster, *et al.* West *Africa since 1800: the Revolutionary Years,* (London: Longman, 1980) p.123.
52. J.F.A. Ajayi, *Christian Missions in Nigeria, 1841-1891: The Making of a New Elite* (Essex: Longman, 1965) p.8.
53. *Ibid.* pp. 31-35.
54. *Ibid.* pp. 35-36.
55. K.O. Dike, *Trade and Politics in the Niger Delta* (Oxford: Clarendon Press, 1956) passim; Cf. Alan Burns, *History of Nigeria* (London: Allen & Unwin, 1981) pp.343-345.
56. Memorandum of Captain John Foote, HMS Madagascar, Senior Officer Commanding the Bights Division, 15 May, 1843.
57. William de Graft to the Methodist Secretary, 4 June & 4 July, 1843.
58. K.U. Idonije, "Badagry and the Missionaries, 1842-1900", (Unpublished B. A. (History) Project, University of Port Harcourt, Nigeria, 1981) p.17; Cf. Ajayi, *Christian Missions in Nigeria,* p.31.
59. A. Babs Fafunwa, *History of Education in Nigeria,* (London: Allen & Unwin (1974) pp.79 & 82.
60. H.H. Johnston cited in E.A. Ayandele, *The Missionary Impact on Modern Africa, 1842-1914: A Social and Political Analysis* (London: Longman, 1991) p. 28.
61. J.S. Mbiti, *African Religions and Philosophy* (New York:Praeger Publishers, 1969) pp.229-241.

62. K.O. Dike and J.F.A. Ajayi, "African Historiography", *International Encyclopedia of the Social Science*, vol.6 (1968). cf. E.J. Alagoa, "African and Western Historiography before 1800", *Storia Della Storiografia*, 19(1991).
63. S.T. Olali, *History of Christianity in West Africa:The Nigerian Experience, 15th-20th Centuries*, (Port Harcourt: The Author, 2002) pp.49-57
64. J.S. Coleman, *Nigeria: Background to Nationalism* (Benin: Broburg & Winston, 1986) pp.175-178
65. O. Kalu, *Christianity in West Africa: the Nigerian Story* (Ibadan: I.U.P., 1978) passim.
66. G.O.M. Tasie, "The Prophet Garrick Sokari Braide of Bakana", in T.N. Tamuno and E.J. Alagoa(eds.) *Eminent Nigerians of Rivers State*(Ibadan: Heinemann, 1980) pp.135-145.
67. E.A. Ayandele, *Holy Johnson: Pioneer of African Nationalism, 1836-1917* (London: Frank Cass, 1970) p. 360.
68. *Ibid.* pp. 358-359
69. Mr. Sokari Braide and Ernest Braide of Bakana in oral accounts at the author's Office, University of Port Harcourt, Nigeria, on 10 November, 1997 and 21 September, 1999, respectively.
70. Ayandele, *Holy Johnson*, p.356
71. Oral evidence of Mr. Samuel N.C. Agwanwo of the Celestial Church of Christ, Choba, on 18 Jan., 2000.

9. Religion, Health & Healing: A Case Study of Prayer Healing & Exorcism among Muslims in Nigeria

Abdulrazaq Kilani
Department of Religious & Cultural Studies, University of Port Harcourt, Nigeria.

Introduction

The practice of casting out evil spirits and prayer healing is not a new development in Islam. However, the wave at which Muslims submit themselves for exorcism from perceive demonic attack and the preponderance at which Muslim groups organize themselves on weekly basis for the recitation of verses of Qur'an and special supplications credited to the Prophet of Islam for protection against demonic attack has been an unprecedented one, especially from the illiterate, semi-literate and the western educated Muslims.

The use of spiritual means like prayer to effect physical and psychosomatic relief is as old as the history of Islam. Healing which means the removal of the factors that cause disease and infirmity and illness is regarded as the physical or psychological loss of harmony. To be healthy therefore is to be adjusted, and the goal of most therapy including prayer and exorcism is to return a person to a satisfactory mode of functioning in society.

There is no gain saying the fact that each culture has its own attitude towards illness and health and that the focus of the healing activity is the whole person whether carryout by a doctor, healer or 'medicine man'. The objective of the research is to investigate the practice of prayer healing and exorcism for the victim of demonic possession among Muslims in Nigeria.

The Relationship between Religion and Healing

Increasing research (Harold G. Koenig, 2002) is demonstrating a positive link between one's faith and the practice of that faith with one's physical and mental health. Religion and health or medicine are no strangers to one another because the two have been strongly linked for ages. This explains why for several hundred years ago, physical disease was understood largely in religious or spiritual terms. Koenig (2002) maintains that artifacts from prehistoric period indicates that mental and physical illnesses were not distinguished from one another, and both were believed to be caused by evil spirits.

The reason for the almost fantastic explosion of interest in healing today apart from economic crisis in many homes, which has led to dislocation in many families, is also due to the need to find a way to live a healthy life in a physical and psychological environment. What it implies is that a physical disorder affects our personality, and what goes on in the personality also affects the health of the body. The whole human being is a remarkable unity of the body, with its various parts and functions and the psyche or personality, with its equally diverse aspects (John A. Sanford.1977:7). The healthy person would thus seem to be the one in whom all these myriad parts are functioning harmoniously. This explains why illness is regarded as the physical or psychological loss of harmony. To be healthy is to be adjusted, and the goal of most therapy is to return a person to a satisfactory mode of functioning in society.

The practice of prayer healing and exorcism among Muslims, which predates the modern era, has been found to be effective in restoring health of the mentally sick people. The effectiveness or otherwise of healing among Muslims just like any religious practice is anchored on faith. Faith which means the total acceptance of a religious system and the person who is able to accept all that is offered to him with little or no doubt, struggling or dissent makes someone a faithful believer. The importance of the study stems from the fact that the various ideological camps among the Muslims are unanimous in the acceptance of the validity of the practice of prayer healing and exorcism. It therefore means that any religious system that can offer total adjustment to life with a diminution of pain and struggle will win an immediate following.

The relationship between religion and health has received the attention of many scholars. Many health professionals argue that religious beliefs and practices have little effect or even adverse effects on mental health and, in some instances, on physical health. Freud has been foremost among scholars to question the religion's benefit and he presented his views on religion and mental health clearly and persistently in his numerous essays. Among the views that is very clear from Freud is his comparison of prayer and religious ritual to the obsessive acts of the neurotic. Albert Ellis and Wendell Watters believe that religious involvement lies at the root of emotional disturbance, low esteem, depression and even schizophrenia (Harold G. Koenig).

The religious climate in Nigeria just like any African community whether Christian, Muslim or Traditionalist is dominated by the belief in spirits which are both malevolent and benevolent. This seems to explain what Adrian Hasting (1976:72) observation thus:

> *They do not for a moment deny the presence of spirits to be cast out, witchcraft spells to be housed, but faced with them they assert the power of God to free and to restore.*

The practice of prayer healing and exorcism has been documented by Muslim scholars from classical period notable in this area was the famous scholar like Ibn Taymiyyah (1263-1328). The compilation of Hadith (sayings of the Prophet) contains numerous incantations and passages from the Qur'an credited to the early generation of Muslims that could be used for exorcism. Notable scholars of Islam like Shaykh Ibn Baaz (late Mufti of Saudi Arabia) acknowledged demonic possession, prayer healing and exorcism in Islamic worldview (Fataawaa, 1988:9-11).

Through the years, religious leaders have been handling psychological dynamite with little awareness of the tremendous power for good or ill in their hands. In recent decades, the behavioural sciences and the psychotherapeutic disciplines, tools for testing the impact of various forms of religion on people's lives, have begun to become available thereby reinforcing people's faith in religious healings.

Demonic Possession and Exorcism in Islam
The issue of possession of man by the *jinn* may appear strange to some people due to lack of information on the matter, but Islam has provided adequate information on the menace in the Qur'an and the Hadith. There are various testimonies from males and females of their experience of sexual intercourse with strange beings mostly in their sleep in Nigeria, which are available to the writer and also a common problem that is often

related by victims. The amazing part of the experience of some of the victims indicate that their "lovers" are mostly from other parts of the world and speak impeccable English in some cases while others speak languages that are not understood by their victims. Bilkis, a 20 year old undergraduate confessed that her visitors are mainly white men probably from Asia, Europe or America. (Oral Interview). A house wife in Port Harcourt who does not understand any other language apart from Hausa was possessed by a *jinn* who claimed to be a native of South Korea (Oral Interview). A Muslim spinster in Lagos experienced having her dirty clothes she packed for washing mysteriously washed and ironed by an unknown person. When exorcism was done on her, a mysterious voice from her mouth indicated that he was doing the washing for her in order to take care of her as a lover (Oral Interview). This experience may not be restricted to the Muslims as most Pentecostal churches in Nigeria anchor their healing crusades and revival on demonic attack, a practice, which hitherto was restricted to the Aladura churches. In medieval Europe there were reported cases of monks and nuns who were visited by voluptuous female demons, which were called *Succubi*. During the period, many nuns became pregnant and killed their children at birth burying them outside the nunneries (Bilal-Philips 31). Many Christian scholars like St Augustine and St Thomas accepted the existence of

Succubi and dealt extensively with the subject. Modern researchers into the experience of the nuns and monks dismissed the idea of the demons as figment of imagination due to their deprivation from sex and that the pregnancies were due to their illicit affairs with other monks and priests (Bilal-Philips 32).

Islam has identified that demonic possession is caused by the activities of satan or the *jinn* and that explains why demonic possession is called the touch of the *jinn* (al-Ashqar 1998: 204). Ibn Taimiyyah (1263-1328), one of the classical scholars of Islam explained the causes of possession by the *jinn*:

> *Possession of the human by the jinn can occur from desires, lusts, passion and zealousness in the same way that a human is in accord with another human...And it also occurs, and this is the majority case, due to hatred and revenge. For example, one of the humans harms a jinn or the jinn thinks that the human was trying to harm them by urinating on some jinn or throwing hot water on them or a human might kill a jinn, even though the human might not have realized that. Among the jinn is ignorance and wrongdoing and, therefore, they get revenge from humans above and beyond what is just. And it could occur from the horseplay or simply evil acts of the jinn in the same way the evil is done by*

the foolish of the humans (Majmoo al-Fataawa, vol. 19. p. 39).

Ibn Baz also opined that the consensus of the Muslim nation acknowledge the possibility of a *jinn* entering a human and possessing him/her. The attitude of Islam to demonic possession is that it is an act of oppression from one being to another being. It is on this basis of this judgment that the act of exorcism is not only recommended but compulsory in order to aid one who is possessed. In Islam helping the oppressed is a duty prescribed on every Muslim according to one's ability. The Prophet recommended to the Muslims the following duties:

> *Al-Barraa' ibn 'Aazib said, Allah's Messenger commanded us to do seven things and prohibited us from doing seven. He enjoined on us visiting the sick, following the funeral processions, wishing well for one who sneezes, fulfilling oaths, helping the oppressed, responding to invitation, and spreading greetings of peace. He forbade the wearing of gold rings, drinking from silver vessels, using silk brocade saddle blankets, wearing silk blend clothes, silk clothes, velvet and silk brocade. (Sahih Bukhari (Arabic–English) vol.8, 156, Muslim (English trans.) vol.3, 1139, no. 5129).*

In another tradition, the Prophet said, "help your brother whether he is the oppressor or the oppressed. Anas asked, "O Messenger of Allah! I would help him if he is oppressed, but how can I help him when he is the oppressor?" He replied, "By preventing him from oppression you are helping" (Sahih Bukhari, vol.3, 373, no 624, Muslim (English trans.) vol. 4, 147, no. 6254). The act of exorcism is considered as a means of alleviating the suffering of another person and the *jinn* that have possessed another person as an oppressor that must be prevented or stopped from oppressing others. Islam therefore provides that if exorcism is to be done by any Muslim it must be based on recommended portions of the Qur'an and such prayers as recommended by the Prophet. Hence, Islam disapproves of incantations (ruqyah) that their meanings are not known or contain words of polytheism (shirk) or unbelief (kufr). Ideological standpoint of Islam is that there are sufficient cures in what has been handed down from the early generations of Muslims from the authentic prayers of the Messenger. The spread of Islam to other parts of the world over the years has brought about certain practices, which are considered very reprehensible in Islam. Among such noticeable practices include magic, talisman, charm, horoscope and divination.

Magic, Charm, Amulet and Islam

The reality of magic is not denied in Islam and there is no disagreement among scholars that learning magic, charms, and amulets and their procurement, as protective devices are unlawful. What has made them to appear, as part and parcel of Islam has been their preponderance in the spiritual landscape of most Muslim societies, especially of Africa. Magic and its related practices go against the very foundation of the scriptural teachings of Islam

The background to magic is the spirit world of *shaitan* (devil) and the disbelieving *jinns*. *Jinns* are intermediate class of beings between man and the angels. The *jinns* according to the doctrine of Islam are beings created with free will, living on earth in a world parallel to that of man, and are invisible to human eyes in their normal state (Bilal Philips, 1) The Qur'an makes reference to magic in Q2:102 as one of the traps of the devil to mislead people from the path of righteousness. Those who practice magic and divination depend on unbelieving *jinns* for information which they use to perform acts that aree considered unIslamic (Q 72:14). The Qur'an 20:69 declares that "And the magician will never be successful whatever amount of skill he may attain". The Prophet condemns magic and fortunetelling when he was reported in Buhkari thus:

> *Aisha narrated that some asked the Apostle of Allah about the fortunetellers. He said," they are nothing". They said, O Allah's Apostle! Sometimes they tell us of a thing which turns out to be true." Allah's Apostle said, A jinn snatches that true word and pours it into the ear of his friend (the fortune teller). The fortune teller then mixes with that word one hundred lies"* (Bukhari Vol 7, p. 439).

Islam, however, made licit the practice of spiritual protection (ruqya) in which the Prophet called evil eyes, prescribes certain chapters of the Qur'an. The recitation of Ayatul-kurisiyy has been recommended by the Prophet to believers as a protection against all forms of evil plots or schemes against any believer. "Whoever reads it" says the Prophet, "Allah will not stop to have a protector for him and Satan will not come closer to him" (Bukhari). Ibn Taymiyyah wrote thus:

> *The numerous people who have experience these events all confirm the amazing effectiveness of this verse warding of devils and breaking their spells. It has a great effect in repelling devils from humans, from the possessed and from those picked out by devils, such as wrongdoers, people with bad tempers, those who follow their desires and lusts... if these verses are read over them with sincerity to Allah, the devils will leave. It*

will put an end to the mirages created by the devils (Majmoo Vol.19, 55)

Evil eye is described by Ibn Khaldun (1967) as psychic influence that is exercised by the soul of the person who is envious. It becomes harmful when someone wants to take away from the owner an object of appreciation (pp 170-171). The place of **ruqyah** cannot be denied in Islam. The Hadith of the Prophet is replete with information on it and an important Hadith in this respect in which Abu Sa'id al-Khudri reported thus:

> *Some of the companions of the Prophet came across a tribe amongst the tribes of the Arabs, and that tribe did not entertain them. While they were in that state, the chief of the tribe was bitten by snake, they said to the companions of the Prophet, have you got any medicine with you or anybody who can treat with ruqyah? The Prophet's companions said, "You refused to entertain us, so we will not treat your chief unless you pay us for it." So they agreed to pay them a flock of sheep. One of the companions started reciting Surat al-Fatihah and gathering his saliva and spitting it at the snake bite. The patient got cured and his people presented the sheep to them but they said, 'We will not take it unless we ask the Prophet (whether it is lawful).' When they asked the Prophet, he smiled and said, "how do you know that*

> *Surat al-Fatihah is a ruqyah? Take it and assign a share for me* (Bukhari vol.7 Hadith nos 632 and 645, pp 424 and 431-3).

What is apparently clear from the Hadith is that, the companions of the Prophet used verses of the Qur'an to treat the sick. Though they charge a fee for the service rendered, Islam has not approved the professionalization of Islam as being practiced by some sections of the Muslim scholars today except for those who establish schools and are involved in the teaching of Islamic sciences to the Muslims. The Qur'an is either an argument for against a person (al- Nawawi, No 23) meaning that if a person turns to it with belief and seeks its guidance; it is a healing and a mercy. According to Ibn Rajab:

> *If someone fulfills Allah's rights upon him, then for him, Allah will take care of all of his needs and interests in this world and the Hereafter. The one who wants Allah to protect, guard and look after all of his affairs should tend to Allah's rights upon him. If a person does not want to face anything that he dislikes, he should not do anything that Allah dislikes him to do* (53).

It is also discernible from Islamic traditions that the frequent mention of the names and attributes of Allah in earnest is considered in Islam as of benefit to the supplicant. The frequent mentioning of the names of Allah cannot be confined to the tongue alone to have the expected benefit for a person but must be accompanied with the heart. There is no gain saying the fact that, there are people who do *dhikr* (God's remembrance) but still feel the effects of Shaytan and its agents. The *dhikr* is like a sword that is in the hand of the warrior, if his arm is strong, he is able to penetrate and kill his enemy but if on the other hand, his arm is weak, he may leave no mark on the enemy. It is apposite to ask at what point should one consider an act licit or illicit?

> *Qatadah said I asked Sa'id b. Musaiyyab, "If a person is betwitched or is unable to have sexual intercourse with his wife, is it permissible to remove the magic effect or use nashra (special kind of treatment)? He said, Yes, there is no harm in it, for it is meant for a good purpose, and what benefits people has not been forbidden* (Bukhari Vol 7, p. 443).

The practice of using ruqya to counter or remove the effect of magic is considered not only good but meritorious and licit in Islam. The term *ruqyah* means to seek protection under the wings of Allah (al-iyad billah) from Shaytan and the evil eye. While the Qur'aan is primarily a book for spiritual remedy, the Muslims also agree that the whole Qur'an is also a protection for the believers and has ability to heal physical ailments (Q 17:82).

There is no doubt that scholars of Islam consider magic as *shirk* (polytheism) and hence illegal and corrupt the monotheistic feature of Islam. In West Africa for example where the practice has been identified as a notable feature of Islam, Al-Maghili recommended that Muslims who practiced magic should be stopped, practitioners should be put to death and deny proper Islamic burial (Owusu- Ansah, 33). The practice of magic Al-Maghili submitted, is heresy and apostacy. The author of *Risalah*, Ibn Abi Zayd al-Qayrawani opined that what is beneficial cannot be kufr (unbelief) and therefore approves such acts for curing impotency, quieting the mind of madman, exorcising *jinn*s and staunching a hemorrhage. Islam has not just considered an act acceptable only on the basis of benefit to people but has also insisted that the method and the prescription must not contradict the monotheistic teaching of Islam. The free- lance nature of amulets and their attendance corruption on the aqeedah (beliefs) of the Muslims must have caused Muslim reformers of the 19th century Hausaland to spend much time and energy in educating the Muslims on aspects of charms and amulets that were consider unIslamic. It is in this respect that the trio of Islamic movement in Nigeria, Usman Dan Fodiyo,

Abdulah Fudi and Muhammad Bello condemned astrology, numerology and forecasting the future as outright unbelief. They however approved and defended the Qur'an and Sunnah as acceptable sources of ruqyah. Quranic and Hadith passages used as ruqyah constitute dua- an unregulated individual or private prayer.

There are references in the book of Hadith, 'Prophetic instructions' on the benefits of some verses and chapters of the Qur'an for the purpose of healing activities or exorcism, which has been passed down from one generation to the other.

Prayer Healing Practices in Nigeria
The practice of prayer healing in Nigeria has been greatly influenced by the preponderant of the concept of evil and other associated beliefs among the various ethnic groups in Nigeria. Islam from inception has also incorporated into its *da'wah* (Islamic propagation) technique healing practice, which is designed to provide alternative to the new convert to Islam. The practice of healing as a vehicle of Islamic propagation cuts across the various ethnic groups where Muslims are found in Nigeria. The non-Muslim neighbours are also a major beneficiary of some Muslim scholars healing power or barakah. A significant proportion of those who embrace Islam in some communities are doing so due to spiritual assistance rendered by Muslim scholars. It should be mentioned

that this trend is not uniformed, as some scholars prefer to collect their fees rather than encourage their clients to embrace the faith. Healing has been use by various Muslim scholars as an important method of Islamic propagation. It is in this respect that Muslim scholars are not seen as mere teachers of Islamic sciences but healers and spiritual consultants.

Healing has been an essential ingredient in creating charisma. Charisma, Weber opines as "the quality of an individual personality by virtue of which he is set apart from other men and treated as empowered with supernatural, superhuman or at least specifically exceptional powers or qualities (358). Islamic healings are therapies identified with Islamic traditions as taught by the Prophet while Muslim healings are therapies introduced by and identified with Muslim scholars which entails the use of Qur'anic texts or merely inverted Qur'anic words and other forms of prayer composed by themselves. A closer look at some of the prayers reveal the robust use of *jinn*s in such invocations, a practice which is against the monotheistic teaching of Islam. The healing therapies are reserved for resolving social problems like success in business, politics, or in romance, infertility, demonic possession, witch attack, bad dream, avoidance of enemies and popularity. It also includes assisting in rejuvenating a dull brain, children crying at night, menstrual irregularity among women, protracted illness during pregnancy and for the attainment of glory, love and honour in the society. There are also those who seek assistance against gunshots, machetes and other dangerous weapons. The assistance to people in this area has, however, produced multiplier effects on the society in that notorious armed robbers, ethnic militia and political thugs atrocities have been linked to such 'spiritual assistance'. It should however be mentioned that, Muslim healers alone are not the only group in Nigeria who render such service to these groups that undermine the peace of the society.

The major practice among the *Malams* involves the writing of Quranic text (Yoruba- *Hantu* and Hausa-*rubutu*) in black wooden slates for drinking or written in paper and wrapped with thread and worn as amulets (Yoruba-*Tira*, Hausa-*Laya*). The traditional ink use in writing in slates or paper is produced by boiling *Oyi* leaves and added with sugar. The sugar is added as a spice because the boiled *Oyi* leaves is very bitter and to make drinking very easy for clients. Most of the writings on wooden slate or paper usually contain what is called *khatim* or seal. The *khatim* are magical squares, which are represented, in a larger square in which other smaller ones are produced in grid patterns. In the smaller squares, Arabic words, letters, numbers and phrases are written. In this process, each of the Arabic letters is represented by certain numerical equivalent. According to Oseni, the popular expression of *Bismi Allah ar-Rahman ar-Raheem* (In the Name of Allah, The Most Gracious, the Most Merciful) is represented with the code number 786/7 (Oseni, 1988:85). The insertions are usually names and attributes of God, His angels, the Prophets and/ or the itemized variable reduced into their numerical values are believed to have the power to effect the efficacy of the amulet (Ansah, 96)

In Islamic healing, power is primarily considered to be from Allah and to be a friend of Allah (wali) or servant (abd), according to Last is to have potential access to that power (187). Scholars accepted into Allah's service after years of apprenticeship, have access not only to that power but also to the knowledge of how to use the powers that Allah has locked into his creations. Muslim healing power appeals to all, illiterate, semi-literate and the learned and this is because the Muslim healing power is still considered peculiarly efficacious by people despite the level of literacy in the society and this explains why clients/customers cut across all the strata of the society. The economic down turn, new commercial demands through global capitalism, easy communication have aided the quest by healers to market their power (barakah) more than before hence contributing significantly to 'the expanding industry of prayer and Islamic medicine.' The prayer economy has been sustained due to the understanding among people that prayer is seen as an adjunct to success, hence Muslim healers readily find attachments to the household, politician, business men and women and professional educated Muslims who want to reach the peak of their careers. It is in this sense that most scholars are noted today for their healing power rather than for their teaching hence the quest of the younger generations who want employment to join the "Sayers of prayers" for money (Last, 196).

Another important feature of healing activities among Muslims in Nigeria is the practice of astrological divination technique (hisab) which determines signs of the zodiac by a mathematical process and not by the date of one's birth. While the practice of divination is a major plank of Muslim healing therapy in which divination is used as a means of diagnosis, Islam considers it as forbidden to use *jinn* to probe into the unseen, treat sickness or even act of fortune telling as therapies of healing. The Prophet was reported to have said, "whoever goes to a fortune-teller and asks him about something, his prayer will not be accepted for forty days" (Muslim). In another tradition, the Prophet was reported to have said "whoever goes to a soothsayer and believes what he says has disbelieved in that which was revealed to Muhammad" (al- Sunnah).

It is also noticeable on closer scrutiny and observation that what most Muslim healers do in the name of

"Islamic healing" are nothing more than witchcraft, sorcery, necromancy, palmistry, star gazing and in some cases, occultism. The consensus of Muslim scholars is that it is permissible to seek treatment for one's ailments. They are allowed to go and consult an expert on every ailment in order to apply the medicines that are permissible for the cure. The ideological position of Islam is that Allah has sent down the disease and has also sent down with it the cure; those who know it know it, and those who do not, do not and that Allah has not created the healing for His creatures in what He has forbidden to them. It is on this basis that going to soothsayer as a healing method or a process of diagnosis is rejected by Islam. It is also unIslamic to summon *jinns* and seek their help in carrying out healing activities, but it is discernible in the activities of most Muslim healers that procuring the assistance of the *jinns* is a major source of healing power and hence supplications prescribed by most healers contain names of *jinns*. A number of ignorant Muslims are seen in mosques and homes chanting the names of *jinns* for invocations and dangerous consequences have been recorded among such people, which cannot be scientifically proven to be due to the chanting of such names of the *jinns*. The testimonies of most victims especially on strange beings that appear to the victims make it not far fetch to conclude that such experience may not be wished away as hallucination but the havoc of *jinn*s.

In the area of divination, striking similarities exist between the Muslim healers' divination method and the Ifa priests. Both divination methods use 'sharp' sand taken from the bank of the ocean or "dry wood powder" or *Iyerosun* among the Yoruba. In the case of Ifa divination, there are sixteen **Odu Ifa** (Ifa Corpus) while Muslim diviners also have equal numbers. The only difference is the name given to them by the different diviners. It is apposite for us to list the names:

Ifa Divination	Muslim Divination
Ejiogbe	Tariki
Oyeku	Jamaa
Iwori	Ijtimaa
Odi	Ashikafu
Irosun	Nasiru Harija
Owonrin	Nasiru Dahila
Obara	Ahayan
Okanran	Inkisi
Ogunda	Utuba Harija
Osa	Utuba Dahila
Ika	Humura
Oturupon	Bayali
Otura	Nakiyalihali

Irete	Kaosaji
Ose	Kabula Harija
Ofun	Kabula Dahila

Source: M.O. Abdul 1970:12.

The divination technique of Muslim healers also includes the use of prayer rosary. A client is asked to pick one rosary bead out of the ninety-nine beads that make the prayer rosary. The diviner examines the number picked by the client and begins to foretell events s/he considers in the future or the nature of the problem that has brought the client to the healer. There are those whose divination is done by looking into water or the palm of the client. An appraisal of the divination techniques of Muslim healers indicates interaction of traditional religious practices with Islam or syncretism. By syncretism, it means the infiltration of a supposedly 'pure' tradition by symbols and meanings seen as belonging to other incompatible traditions (Shaw and Stewart, 1). Muslim healers have been involved in the politics of religious synthesis by making elements of two different historical traditions to interact and even combine. The divination practices of healers in Islam run contrary to the anti-syncretistic telos of Islam (Fisher, 1973, 1985). There are some scholars of Islam who are not professional healers but provide assistance to Muslims who are victims of demonic possession and those who need spiritual assistance in general. This group of scholars adheres to prescriptions of Prophet Muhammad (saw) on such spiritual problems.

In the study of Hadith of the Prophet, there are references on how a Muslim can attend to the problem of evil eyes, demonic possession and magic without being guilty of shirk. Those prescriptions were recorded from the authentic sayings of Prophet Muhammad. It is apposite to enumerate some of these prescriptions:

(i) Seeking refuge with Allah from the *jinn*, Allah says in Qur'an 41:36 "And if an evil whisper from Shaytan tries to turn you away (from doing good), then seek refuge in Allah. Verily, He is the All Hearer, the All knower." Also in Qur'an 7:200 "And if an evil whisper comes to you from Shaytan, then seek refuge with Allah. Verily, He is All- Hearer, All knower."

(ii) Reciting al- Mi'wadhatayn (the last two chapters of the Qur'an, al-Falaq and Naas). It was narrated that Abu Sa'eed al–Khudri said : "The Messenger of Allah used to seek refuge with Allah from the evil eye until the Mi'wadhatayn were revealed, and when they were revealed he started to recite them and nothing else." (Tirmidhi, 2058 and authenticated as saheeh by Albani in *Saheeh al-Jaami* 4905).

(iii) Reciting Aayat al-Kursiy. It was narrated that Abu Hurayrah said:

> *The Messenger of Allah put me in charge of guarding the Zakaah of Ramadaan. Someone came to me and started grabbing handfuls of the food. I took hold of him and said, 'I will take you to the Messenger of Allah.' He said 'I will teach you some words by means of which Allah will benefit you.' I said' What are they?' He said, 'When you go to bed, recite "the verse of the throne". Then Allah will appoint a guard for you who will stay with you and no Shaytaan (devil) will come near you until morning.' The Messenger of Allah asked me 'What did your prisoner do last night?' I said, 'O Messenger of Allah, he taught me something, and claimed that Allah would benefit me by it.' He said, 'What was it?' I said, 'He taught me to recite Aayat al-kursiy when I go to bed, and said that no Shaytaan would come near me until morning, and that Allah would appoint a guard for me who would stay with me.' The Prophet said, 'he told you the truth, although he is an inveterate liar. That was the Shaytaan"* (Bukhari, 3101).

(iv) Reciting Surat al- Baqarah. It was narrated from Abu Hurayrah that the Messenger of Allah said: "Do not make your houses like graves, for the Shaytaan runs away from a house in which Surat al-Baqarah is recited (Muslim, 780).

(v) The last two verse of Surat al-baqarah. It was narrated that Abu Mas'ood al-Ansari said: "The Messenger of Allah said: 'Whoever recites the last two verses of Surat al-Baqarah at night, that will suffice him" (Bukhari, 4723, Muslim, 807). In another narration, the Messenger said "if the last two verses of Baqarah are recited for three nights, no Shaytaan (devil) will remain in the house" (Tirmidhi 2882 classed as Saheeh by Albani in *Saheeh al Jaami*, 1779).

(vi) Remembering Allah often (dhikr). It was narrated from al-Haarith al- Ash'ari that the Prophet said: "Allah commanded Yahyah ibn zakariyah five things to follow and to enjoin upon the children of Israel... and he commanded them to remember Allaah, and the likeness of that is a man who was being pursued by the enemy, until he reached a strong fortress in which he found protection; similarly a man cannot find protection from the Shaytaan except by remembering Allaah..." (al-Tirmidhi, 2863 and classed Saheeh by Albani in *Saheeh al-Jaami* 1724).

(vii) Reciting the Qur'an offers protection against the shaytaan. Allah says in the Qur'aan "And when you recite the Qur'aan, We put between you and those who believe not in the hereafter, an invisible veil" (Qur'aan 17:45).

(viii) The adhaan or call to prayer. Abu Hurayrah also narrated that the Messenger of Allah said, "When the Shaytaan hears the call to prayer, he runs away fast" (Muslim, 389).

The teaching of Islam on healing is anchored on the understanding that good health is essential in order to fulfill the obligation of the religion and worship Allah. It is in this respect that Islam prescribes to the Muslims to act according to what is prescribed in the Qur'an and the Sunnah and avoid things that are considered forbidden. The art of healing is not a mere result of good luck but the outcome of the mercy of Allah: "And when I am sick, then He heals me"(Qur'an 26:80). If we consider health as a physical condition in which all the functions are healthy, a good health is the best gift of Allah to man. The Prophet (SAW) brought out the importance into fore when he said, "There are two gifts of which many men are cheated-good health and leisure" (Suyyuti,6). In addition, he was reported to have said, "whoever awakes in the morning with a healthy body, and a self that is sound, and whose provision is assured, he is like the one who possesses the whole world" (Suyyuti). Islam recognizes the weakness of man just like the general saying that to err is human but to forgive is divine, Prophet Muhammad (SAW) advised the Muslims "ask Allah for forgiveness and health. After certainty of faith, nothing better is given to a man than good heath" (Suyyuti, 7).

Conclusion

The pertinent question is why people patronise Muslim healers in view of the modern medical facilities around the country. One of the reasons is the strong tie people have cultivated in religion and the preponderance of religion in all facets of human endeavour. In addition to this, any prolonged illness or misfortune is believed to be inflicted by spiritual forces and can only be subdued by spiritual therapy. The general belief is that medical science does not have explanation for such ailments. There are instances when a patient has been taken to the hospital is found to have stayed more than necessary, such patient is withdrawn and taken to Muslim healers and became healed. Politicians, students and contractors due flock the houses of healers for help in order to achieve their desire goals in life. The menace of fake drugs importation from India, China and other countries of Asia by unscrupulous Nigerian merchants has also contributed to the patronage the healers are receiving from the people. There is no gain saying the fact that young Muslim intellectuals with ideological leaning to *"Salafiyyah"* are educating the people on what they consider the unorthodox methods of most of these healers. The success or otherwise of their efforts are discernible in the society but it is still low as compared to the popularity of the healers in the society. The healing therapy of the Muslims in Nigeria has an age long tradition and the clients cut across religion, class or ethnicity. It should also be noted that the healing therapy was a vehicle of Islamic propagation in most Nigeria society.

References

Abdul, M.O.A, "Yoruba Divination and Islam" *Orita: Ibadan Journal of Religious Studies*, No. 4, 1970.

Albani, *Saheeh al- Jami al- Sagheer* (Beirut: Maktabal-Islami, 1986).

As-suyyuti, Abdur-Rahman, *As-Suyyuti's Medicine of the Prophet*, Ta-Ha Publishers; Ltd, London, 1997.

Bilal Philips, Abu Ameenah, *Ibn Taymiyyah's Essay on The Jinn (Demons)* (NP, ND).

Bercher, L, (trans. and ed.) *Risalah Ibn Abi Zayd al-Qayrawani*, Alger 1945.

Clinebell, J. Howard Jr. *Mental Health through Christian Community* (Abingdon, 1965).

Fisher, H.J., ' Conversion reconsidered: Some Historical aspects of Religious Conversion in Black Africa' *Africa*, vol. 43, 1973, pp. 27-40.

Hasting, Adrian, *Christianity in Africa* (London: Geoffrey Chapman, 1976).

Harold, T. Christensen, *Handbook of Marriage and the Family*, Chicago: Rand McNally and co, 1964, p. 441.

Hobhouse, L.T. *Morals in Evolution: A study of Comparative Ethics*, London: Chapman and Hall, 1951, p213),

Ibn Baaz, Abdul Azeez, *Fataawa on Refutation of Those Who Deny Demonic Possesion* (Riyadh: Ad-Da'wah al-Islaameeyah as- Sahafeeyah Co., 1408/1988)

Ibn Khaldun, *The Muqaddimah: An Introduction to History* trans. Franz Rosenthal, Princeton 1967, pp. 170-171

Ibn Rajab, Abdul Rahman, *Noor al-Iqtibaas fi Mishkaat Wasiyyah al-Nabiyy li-ibn Abbaas*. Beirut: Daar al-Bashaair al- Islamiyyah, 1989.

Khan, Muhsin, (trans.) *Sahih al Bukhari Arabic-English*, Dar al-Fikr.

Koenig, G. Harold *et al, Handbook of Religion and Health* (Oxford: Oxford University Press, 2001).

Koenig, G. Harold, "Recovering Religion's Ancient Role in Health" *Research News & Opportunities*, July/August, Vol. 2, 2002, p.6

Last, Murray "Charisma and Medicine in Northern Nigeria" in D. Cruise O'Brien and C. Coulon (eds.), *Charisma and Brotherhood in African Islam* (Oxford: Oxford University Press, 1988).

Max Weber, *The Theory of Social and Economic Organization*. Trans. Talcott Parsons, New York: The Free Pres, 1947

Oseni, Z.I. "Islamic Scholars as Spiritual Healers in a Nigeria Society: An examination of the Activities of Mallams in Afemai area of Bendel State" *Islamic Culture*, Vol. LXII, No. 4, pp. 75-88.

Sanford, A. John, *Healing and Wholeness* (NewYork: Paulist Press, 1977).

10. The Fall Story of Genesis 3: The Experience of the Culture of Alienation, Anxiety & Violence

Vincent G. Nyoyoko
Department of Religious & Cultural Studies, University of Port Harcourt, Nigeria.

Introduction

The story of the Fall (Genesis 3) is pivotal in understanding the prevalence of sin, and specifically the experience of the culture of alienation, anxiety and violence in society. For a contextual understanding of this pericope, the scenario must be put in its proper perspective. In this scenario, therefore, Adam and Eve are created good and enjoy immediate knowledge, perfect happiness and friendship with God. When they misuse their gift of freedom and refuse to accept their creaturely status, sin emerges in the world introducing in the process the culture of alienation, anxiety and violence. The paradise becomes a hell. Through the sin of Adam and Eve humanity lost the spiritual and bodily privileges with which men were endowed by God. This sin which is prior to any personal sin affects every man and woman at the moment of their coming into being. Humanity is no longer oriented to the good. Desire, a natural tendency becomes after the Fall an enslaving concupiscence. Under the influence of Augustine, concupiscence has come to be portrayed in Catholic and Protestant theology as a perverse inner tendency to sinful cravings, part of the tragic legacy of the Fall of humanity's primeval first parents. Only the grace of God in Christ Jesus can free humanity

This essay begins by questioning this scenario, and the assumptions which still underline twenty-first century Catholic and Protestant theology. Thereafter, the essay will discuss the creation narrative and the symbol of the Fall in the light of the concerns of the Yahwistic author and the experience of Israel's history. In exploring the meaning of the narrative in the context of our own lives today we will then discuss the experience of the culture of alienation, anxiety and violence, and the factors that complicate our choosing between good and evil. Finally, we will discuss the meaning of Christ's incarnation which effects a radical change in human existence.

The paradise narrative does not point to a state of lost innocence. Rather, it challenges men and women to assume responsibility for the existence of sin in the world, and the structures of violence and exploitation that dehumanize people's lives. It also challenges people to look forward in hope to the final fulfilment of the kingdom, to "what no eye has seen, nor ear heard, nor the heart of man (*or woman*) conceived, what God has prepared for those who love him" (1 Cor 2:9).

Repositioning our Misconceptions

Five issues will be considered here. First, we will endeavour to resolve the traditional conception regarding the story of Genesis 3 as a story of an actual Fall of the first couple into sin. It should be observed here that the narrative nowhere teaches Genesis 3 as a story of the Fall. In fact, nothing could be more remote from the narrative. The story is not in actual fact a myth of falling into sin and guilt, for the word Fall is foreign to biblical vocabulary. It must be stated here that it is only what has been elevated that can fall.[1] It must be added that it is not even a catastrophe which has befallen an innocent creation through a first couple, a once-upon-a-time story when our ancestors were perfect, self-aware and God-conscious; then they made a sinful choice, and because of it little children are already guilty in their mother's womb: then we all become bad. The creation story in Gen. 2:4b-25 does not give us the pessimistic view of human nature that we think it does. It is only in prophets like Hosea and Jeremiah that we have such impressions.

Genesis 3 is a theological critique of the culture of anxiety. It is a comment on the ontological insecurity that derives from freedom. The man and the woman are controlled by their anxiety, the anxiety of possibility, and they seek to escape it by circumventing God and securing their own autonomy and well-being. Thus, the failure to trust God brings death, and death results in the loss of life. It brings discord and disintegration, tension and tragedy. Life and death are the subjects of the narrative and life means unity, harmony, and fulfilment. This situation means centring one's life in God.

The Genesis 3 narrative has been very much misunderstood and misinterpreted. This results from traditional theological stance which takes the story literally and in the process speculates about Adam as a supernaturally perfect human being before the Fall and thereby makes him a stranger to our human condition. Additionally, the vivid pictures of two frightened semi-naked creatures cuddled together outside the gates of paradise, vainly hoping to recapture the security they have left behind, leave lasting imprints on young imaginations. It should be noted that nowhere in the story does it say that the first couple sinned. Literal interpretations which treated the primeval narrative as scientific history, and confused it with later interpretations of Original Sin, particularly that of Augustine have done intellectual harm to generations of Christians. Since the narrative itself is enveloped with ambiguity, it has produced multiple interpretations. It should be borne in mind that it is most anachronistic at this point in time to read Augustine's position on Original Sin back into the narrative.

The second issue revolves around seeing Genesis 3 as a story about the origin of death. Traditional theology sees the narrative as an account of the origin of death in the world. This assumption is based on the mechanistic connection between sin and death. The Bible does not reflect on such a question in any sustained way, for it is not interested in theoretical or abstract questions of sin, death or evil. It is concerned rather with faithful responses and praxis. Death itself is fundamental to the human life God wills for humankind. It should be noted that no one dies in the story. It simply says, "You are dust and unto dust you shall return" (Gen. 3:19). This in no way means that death is punishment for sin. In the very next verses (Gen 3: 20-24), Eve is called the mother of the living. The Hebrew Bible regards death as the natural destiny of all humans. Death is a practical necessity, otherwise the world would become over-populated. Men and women have to leave room for their descendants. In people's desperate search for immortality they have come to see death as an obstacle to be overcome. But there is no natural and tranquil departure, no peaceful passing toward immortal existence. In death, the gateway to the final state of union, people's present state of self-awareness is dissolved.

The third issue has to do with seeing the story as referring to sex and the evil wrought by sex. In Gen. 3:1-7, which is one of the masterpieces of Old Testament literature, the woman discusses theology with a very resilient and intelligent serpent. There is no hint in the story that the serpent is the principle or embodiment of sin. According to Gerhard von Rad, "the mention of the snake is almost incidental".[2] Walter Brueggemann agrees that whatever the serpent may have meant in earlier versions of the story, in the present narrative it has no independent significance. It is merely one of the players in the drama. He adds: "It is a technique to move the plot of the story. It is not a phallic symbol or Satan or a principle of evil or death".[3] It is subtle, cunning and clever but it is a creature and at best it can only tempt. It is up to the responsible agent to yield or resist. Additionally, 'Knowing good and evil' nowhere in the Bible or in any ancient literature refers to sexual knowledge. Brueggemann, therefore, warns that to focus on the linkage between sex and sin is not faithful to the drama.[4] We should rather realize that knowledge is power; it leads to freedom and to the capacity to control.

Genesis 2 states that in God's garden there was mutuality and equality but in Genesis 3 hierarchy and division replace mutuality. The phrase, 'Bone of my bone, flesh of my flesh' is the perfect but impossible union for which man and woman crave, but sexuality is perverted, the man dominates, and both live in unresolved tension (Gen 3: 16c). In this sense, "his supremacy is neither a divine right nor a male prerogative. Her subordination is neither a divine decree nor the female destiny".[5] Thus, it is with the political dynamics of power, control and autonomy that this text is concerned when it refers to the relationship between the sexes. And such control and distortion is not the will of the Creator.

In the fourth instance, we intend to find out if Genesis 3 refers to God punishing the first couple. We may begin this exploration by saying that the tree of life in Mesopotamia is a legendary plant conferring immortality. The "tree of knowledge of good and evil" means totality of knowledge, and has the same meaning as 'like God, knowing good and evil' (Gen 3:5). When the couple's dream of unlimited knowledge and independence is shattered, their eyes are opened and they are naked. Their relationship with God and their own relationship of trust and harmony is also disoriented. Yet nowhere in the story does God directly curse the woman or the man, nor are they abandoned by God. In Gen 3:8, after they have misused their freedom and experienced disharmony, God continues to walk with them in the cool of the evening and enters into dialogue with the confused couple. In Gen 3:21 God even supports them and makes clothes for them.

The fifth issue revolves around seeing in the text the fact that work is a curse that came after the Fall. Historically, the Christian tradition has focused on the concept of work as a curse God inflicted on the earth, and on the two original human beings. In this sense, work has been separated from the goodness of tilling and keeping, from the dignity of co-creating, from responsibility for the goodness of creation. Work has become punishment. Phyllis Trible states that "since the garden of Eden is a place of delight, to till and to keep it is to foster pleasure".[6] She interprets 'to till' and 'to serve' with the connotation of respect, reverence and worship. Work, from the beginning, as depicted in Genesis 2, is an expression of the dignity and integrity of the person. It is not, therefore, a curse that comes with the Fall. Through work, human life shifts from passivity to participation, uniting *ha adam* and *ha adama*, creature and soil.

Explaining the Narrative

The Genesis 3 narrative is set in the context of a myth. Myth in this sense means that the story receives its form before any recorded history. It is from this context that the Genesis 3 narrative is often treated as though it were an explanation of how sin entered the world. The Old Testament is never interested in such an abstract issue and makes no theoretical statement about the origin of sin. The narrative does not even give an explanation for sin. Rather it attempts to separate the origin of sin from the origin of good. Creation had its origin in the creative act of God "and God saw that it was good" (Gen 1:4). The narrative traces the origin of sin not to creation but to an ancestor of the human race. The origin of sin is not woven into the fabric of being, for creation is good, not sin. Sin is not even older than creation, nor contemporary with the origin of things. Sin is the corruption that occurs within creation.

For Paul Ricoeur the intention of the myth "is to set up a radical origin of evil as distinct from the more primordial origin of the goodness of things".[7] It traces the beginning of sin not to the world or its creator but to human beings "in the bosom of creation which has already had an absolute beginning in the creative act of God".[8] The narrative posits a beginning of sin as distinct from the beginning of creation that is already complete and good.

The narrative of Genesis 3 also reveals the mysterious aspect of sin, namely, that before man initiates or commits sin he discovers it already there. Man does not begin sin, rather he continues it. It has its own history, its own past, before man ever becomes implicated in it. As human beings, people are destined for the good and inclined to sin: "in this paradox of 'destination' and 'inclination' the whole meaning of the symbol of the Fall is concentrated".[9] Sin is a reality antecedent to every awakening of consciousness; it has a communal dimension that cannot be reduced to individual responsibility; and it is a power that binds people and holds them captive.[10]

The Yahwist, reflecting on the origin of the chosen people, would have used this primeval narrative to explain the common ancestry of the different ethnic groups. Adam, the mythical figure, provides a focal point at the beginning of history long before Abraham or the patriarchs, or before the people of Israel were divided into many tribes. In Adam all are one. The text itself may be reflecting the concerns in the time of Solomon. The Yahwistic tradition critiques the life situation in Solomon's time, and explains existing realities as sentences meted out by God. The serpent's crawl, the birth pains of woman, her subordinate status in mid-Eastern society, the monotonous nature of work and the drudgery of the peasant's life are explained by him as consequences of sin, - the first couple's Original Sin. It should be added here that the repressive treatment of women cannot be based on scripture any more than the practice of slavery. In Gen 3:15 the seed of the serpent will struggle violently with every generation of humans.

The narrative must also be understood in the light of the historical experience of the Jewish people whose journey was one of fidelity and infidelity, revolt and repentance, captivity and return, judgement and mercy. For C.H. Dodd the primary function of the narrative of Adam and Eve is that of extending to the human race the tragic experience of the exile:

> *It is the tragic fate of Israel projected upon mankind as a whole. The Word of God that drove man out of paradise is the word of judgement that sent Israel into exile, now given a universal application.* [11]

However, Adam is not an important figure in the Hebrew Scriptures, and when he is mentioned, it is without allusion to the story of Genesis 3. The prophets never mention him. Abraham, our father in faith, and Noah, the father of all humankind as recreated after the flood, are much more important figures. The narrative of Genesis 3 must be studied in the context of the Genesis 1-11 narratives which lead to the call of Abraham. For the Jewish believer the narrative supported his twofold belief: the absolute goodness and perfection of God on the one hand, and on the other the sinfulness of human beings.

In the New Testament Jesus never quotes the Adamic narrative for an interpretation of the beginning of sin. He does not understand sin as a residue of some primal crime but recognizes its existence in people's lives and calls for repentance and conversion of heart: "Unless you repent you shall all likewise perish" (Lk. 13:3). It was Paul's Christology that consolidated the Genesis 3 story into a contrast between the 'old man' and the 'new man'. He sets up the figure of Adam in contrast to that of

Christ whom he calls the second Adam (1 Cor 15:21-22, 45-49; Rom 5:12-18). This becomes the context for us.

Rediscovering the meaning of the Narrative

With 'the knowledge of good and evil' the first couple is no longer 'blind' for 'their eyes are opened'. They begin the process of the culture of individuation and cut their ties with nature.

> *With the expulsion from Paradise, the original unity was broken. Man acquired self-awareness and awareness of his fellow man as a stranger in the world. Becoming a stranger, however, does not mean becoming a sinner, and even less being corrupted.* [12]

History now begins. Being part of nature and yet transcending it causes conflict and suffering, and man and woman are driven to find ever new solutions to this conflict. The conflict is solved by experiencing a split between people as subjects and the world as object, a split that cannot be overcome until its existence is acknowledged. Only when people experience themselves as strangers in the world, estranged from themselves and nature can they again become one with themselves, with nature, and with other human beings on a higher level. People achieve harmony by becoming fully human and striving to be one with all of life. Adam and Eve experienced conflict not because they were primitive or ignorant but because they were seeking divine status and becoming the source of their own meaning. In a sense, therefore, the fall of any human person is a consciousness explosion, an awakening, a tasting of infinity. [13] Correspondingly, people's initial consciousness explosion becomes here their first step into mystery, their first taste of infinity, for the birth of consciousness is also the dawning of God-awareness. Their self-transcending spirit opens up infinite possibilities for all: "I set before you this day, life and death, good and evil, choose life…" (Deut 30:15).

The creation narrative points to the rise in human consciousness, the awaking out of paradise into self-awareness. The price of self-awareness is loneliness, anxiety, alienation. It demands that people make choices, and choice is lonely, for it is with the knowledge that there is good and evil, that choice has to be made at all. By affirming their right to choose, Adam and Eve became adults. The first act of disobedience can then be traced to the beginning of human history, because it is the beginning of human freedom.[14] This rests on the fact that freedom is always constrained by its own finitude. It is always hindered by an inescapable anxiety which makes humans vulnerable to sin. But it must be observed here that fallibility, finitude and anxiety are not the consequences of a primal Fall; they are constituents of what it means to be human. Therefore, "we ought to cease understanding the confrontation with the authority of the father, this cutting of the umbilical cord, as sin..."[15] The narrative necessarily mirrors the guilt people experience in growing up, making their own choices, leaving the commanding father, the safety of the womb and their symbiotic life within it. Let me add here that there is no painless or guilt-free path to adulthood and like Adam and Eve people too must journey out into the world, despite their intense longing to stay at home. People must break out of the cosmic, psychic womb, the nourishing waters of paradise, to discover themselves in a world inhabited by spirits, friendly and malevolent.[16] In adulthood, work and sexuality, though given with creation, take on a different and more complex meaning.

The story of humanity's mythic ancestors is less about lost innocence than incompleteness. People experience this incompleteness, this estrangement from their essential being that marks their existence. Life has already become problematic for humans long before they ever make their first conscious decision. Their lives too are criss-crossed with pain and anxiety and sometimes with a sense of frustration and worthlessness. Theology has begun to employ the insights of Freudian psychoanalytic theory of the structure and development of personality, so it realizes that there is no need to appeal to a Fall from a superior state to explain the *id-ego* conflict.[17] Instead of lamenting an imagined lost paradise, humans now live in hope for the final integration of their personalities.

Psychologists tell us[18] that birth and childhood trauma, and the conflicting relationship with parents, may shatter people's world of security and meaning before they can handle these experiences which jolt them into a new world. These alienating experiences cause anxiety and may diminish their sense of self worth. In these situations, people lamentingly internalize their personal disvalue, and in their craving for wholeness they anxiously and aggressively seek power and domination, often at the expense of others. The result is often a tragic incapacity for loving either the good within themselves or in others. It is this defective situation which makes men vulnerable to sin. Since sin in turn brings guilt, men see themselves as unworthy of God's love and become preoccupied with seeking forgiveness. Because men neither believe in themselves, nor in their own self-worth, they seek their personal value from their work and from the recognition they get from others. In the desire to be appreciated and gain control, people generally get caught in the web of the evil structures to which they themselves have contributed. This in turn influences their moral decisions. In a world of structured sins and exploitation men have become tragic victims of their own anxiety. Their negative values and meanings, and that of their culture, are passed on to the next generation who unconsciously absorb and internalize them. And so the choices of every future generation are influenced by the grace and sin which capacities are locked in a struggle whose outcome hangs in the balance. Thus, St. Paul could say, "Where sin increased, grace abounded all the more" (Rom. 5:20).

From the foregoing and in coming to terms with the problem of evil, Eric Neumann urges men to probe the insights of depth psychology and "the paradoxical secret of transformation itself"[19] which challenge people to accept the sin within themselves, to accept their shadow – that unconscious negative part of their personality through which they experience themselves as creatures of a creator who made light from darkness. Only then, he says, will people realize that opposites are linked together as they are in the Godhead, and only then "will the unity of creation and of human existence escape that disastrous rift which threatens the future of the human race"[20].

The Constant Temptation to shun Responsibility

In making choices people may either struggle frantically for the most challenging option, or settle for mediocrity, a false security. The temptation is to want to crawl back into the safety of the womb, to remain in their original paradise. Even before the story of the expulsion from paradise, the Biblical text talks about the necessity of cutting the bond to father and mother: "Therefore a man leaves his father and mother and cleaves to his wife, and they become one flesh" (Gen 2:24). As they leave the garden the first couple leaves behind a phase of their existence.

Adam's most passionate striving, if one could read into his mind correctly, would be to return to the world of union which was his home before he 'disobeyed'. His desire would have been to give up reason, self-awareness, choice, responsibility, and to return to the womb, to Mother Earth, to the darkness where the light of conscience and knowledge does not yet shine. He would have wanted to escape from his newly gained freedom and to lose the very awareness which makes him human.[21]

What people do with their freedom is largely determined by their social milieu, for there is no sealed wall between themselves and culture. People come into a world that has already been shaped by the sinful decisions of others and by sinful situations, the responsibility which cannot really be laid on anyone individually, but can be laid on everyone collectively. It is difficult, therefore, to do consistently what conscience commands.

Christ's Incarnation as the transfusion of new Life and new Energy

Christianity asserts categorically that the incarnation is the renewal, the transformation of all the energies and powers of the universe. It also adds that the Divine Indwelling was already present in the universe long before Jesus ever entered history. And gradually as Jesus came to realize that he and the Divine Indwelling are one, he opened up a whole new understanding of human destiny. This was an extraordinary breakthrough for the universe and for all humanity. Because of this, people now become part of the reign of the divine in history and consequently participate in its mystery. The situation thus provides enough reason to live in gratitude and ecstatic joy. Jesus tells us to claim our divinity, to lay hold of that energy and power within us and to participate in the work of creation. If we do this, his father will love us, and they will come to us and make their home with us (Jn 14:23). Because of this union of God in Christ with the whole of humankind, no area of human existence, whether physiological or psychological is left untouched or unaffected by God's grace. The incarnation then, is not just a prelude to redemption, it is God's intervention as mercy; God's compassion become flesh. It is tantamount to "a transfusion of new life, new energy, and new hope into the bloodstream of the already existing arteries of humankind". [23]

I want to observe that traditional Catholic theology with its emphasis on redemption of the human race has not reflected sufficiently on this mystery and therefore men and women have continued to have an unhealthy preoccupation with guilt and personal sin. Theology needs to emphasise that because the Incarnation is an ongoing reality, the radical healing of God's grace goes even beyond people's personal sins. This healing goes down to the deepest levels of men's psyche, to the very roots of their being. The blocks and barriers, the fears and frustrations that cripple and prevent people from believing in themselves or in their own personal worth, and from being fully alive, can and must be healed. People may experience that grace because of someone else's compassionate living is capable of expressing life lived with human meaning and possessed of real life and commitment. The influence of such a caring person can set free the constructive energy within men and women so that they may allow that energy to transform itself into compassion. The Incarnation, therefore, becomes a continuing mystery in the lives of people and in the world they occupy, and God's grace thereby consecrating them, releasing a new energy within them and inviting them to be fully alive, free and responsive. It was in such a situation that St. Paul could say, "God's love has been poured into our hearts through the Holy Spirit which has been given to us" (Rom 5:5).

Conclusion

The global greenhouse crisis warns us to understand that our personal survival depends entirely on the collective will of humanity. In a world where patriarchal models of domination, global warfare and militarism, starvation and poverty dominate, the world needs nurturing, creativity and healing. It also needs the capacity for understanding and love. While human language, worldview, values and preferences are already moulded and shaped by exploitative economic structures and unjust political systems, these need not control people's lives. Men and women may not take a neutral position, for all of life is good and meaningful and awaits its final fulfilment. The paradise myth points, not to a golden age of the past but to the future kingdom of God, a creation transformed according to the heart of God where "death shall be no more, neither shall there be mourning nor crying nor pain" (Rev. 21:4), for the new heaven and new earth shall have arrived (Rev. 21:1).

People necessarily find harmony and oneness with the world, not by regressing to the pre-human state, but by the full development of their specifically human qualities: love, understanding, compassion. The goal of people's development is that of freedom and autonomy, which demands the cutting of the umbilical cord and the ability to take responsibility for their existence. This introduces men and women to a long lonely journey, and genuine freedom and independence in this context remains a difficult achievement. Generally, people like to hold on to security, to power, to family, to achievements, to certainty. It should also be added here that independence is not achieved by not obeying mother, father, or authority. It is possible only if, and according to the degree to which, people actively grasp the world, are related to it, and thus become one with it. In this state, men and women can grow into the true splendour of affectionate, imaginative persons, living in ecstatic enjoyment of the universe and of shared understanding and compassion with one another.

Historically, within the Christian tradition people have separated God's creation from human work, and therefore they have not been able to see the relationship between God and the worker mediated through work. Work, and the monotony that often accompanies it, has often been seen as the result of Original Sin and the worker instead of being given his/her dignity has often been belittled and humiliated. In feudal and capitalist economies where work has been associated with money, the experience of work has become increasingly one of futility and meaninglessness because people value it only for its earning power. The worker is simply defined by the income he or she receives for services rendered. Work is often done in a degrading environment which offers few opportunities for the worker to explore his or her potential, or creativity. Work has become alienated labour. Only a humanizing, liberating theology of work can appreciate that Adam and Eve did not undo creation. Creation continues after the Fall and men being made in God's image means their becoming co-creators with God in this world. Accordingly, "by caring for creation we pass on the gift of life, and in the process our spirit is passed on as well. It becomes part of the everlasting continuum that binds together all of the countless gifts of life into a single indivisible web".[24] And, as has been observed, this narrative certainly is not the story of the Fall of man and woman but of their awakening and thus the beginning of their rise.

From our discussion so far, Paradise is the dream and not the memory[25] of humanity's primal kingdom. Paradise is the end, not at the beginning; hope longs not for restored innocence but for healing and home in the kingdom. Genesis does not contrast the way things are with the way things were, but with the way they ought to be. The garden is the dream, not the memory. Therefore, according to Stephen Duffy, "For Adam, no superman, is the archetypal representative of all humans and his condition is that of everyone. There never was a time of primal innocence. Paradise is God's own personal garden, where we have never been".[26]

Generally, human beings desire to be one and whole in consciousness as once they were in preconsciousness.

But we must agree that there is no simple return to a pre-awareness condition. Theologically, the angel with the flaming sword (Gen. 3:24) will not allow anyone to re-enter the garden for that would involve the loss of self-awareness, a regression to the pre-individualist harmony with nature. There can be no going back to that pre-awareness state, only a going forward to the glory that lies ahead. Humanity is now a new creation (2 Cor 5:17) and people are being changed into his likeness from one degree of glory to another; for this comes from the Lord who is the Spirit (2 Cor 3:18).

Once men and women come to appreciate the richness within their own personalities, and that by God's grace they have the capacity to love and to live in profound interior communication with one another and with the universe, they can live as compassionate and caring people, intoxicated with enthusiasm for life and its challenges. Since men and women are made in God's image they are called to become the likeness of God, to become centres of creative energy and power for one another and for their agonizing world and cosmos. It is for this reason that people whatever their state in life must creatively "choose life. . ." (Deut. 30:15), and all that it implies.

For contemporary Christians, the future paradise is the kingdom, and men and women enter it through the necessary passage of death. The way of the cross is the only way that leads to the final unfolding and completion of God's love in the world. Jesus has arisen from the dead and now lives forever. Through his resurrection, not only was the hidden glory of his earthly life and death made manifest but the situation of the world was essentially changed. The new life in Christ of which Paul speaks is a life without estrangement. In the Christological hymn of Philippians 2, Christ's exaltation has also brought about the overthrow of the cosmic forces. It has effected a radical change in human existence. Therefore, "Divine wisdom and goodness saves humankind, not through forceful removal of evil, but by the mystery of compassionate suffering whereby evil is transformed into good"[27].

In the New Testament the resurrection is indissolubly linked to the virtue of Christian hope. Thus St. Peter could boldly exclaim, 'Praise be to the God and Father of our Lord Jesus Christ, who in his great mercy gave us new birth into a living hope by the resurrection of Jesus Christ from the dead" (1 Pt. 1:3). It is this hope which makes the future present and gives meaning to the suffering of men and women today. It is in this hope too that today men and women could ponder with St. Augustine on the excellence of divine love when he states: "The all good, all powerful God would not ever allow anything evil in his works unless he was so good and so omnipotent that he could turn evil into good"[28].

And again when he writes: "God judged it better to make good out of evil than to refuse to allow any evil at all". [29]

The origin of sin is not woven into the fabric of being, nor is sin an unbreakable, cyclic recurrence of domination and oppression as Friedrich Nietzsche maintained.[30] Christ has taken on humanity's sins and in the process men and women have received divine forgiveness. Through sacramental incorporation into Christ's death and resurrection people experience here and now the power of the resurrection – a foretaste of their own risen life, as St. Paul would say, "Your real life is Christ and, when he appears, then you too will appear with him and share his glory" (Col 3:3).

Notes and References

1. Paul Ricoeur, *The Symbolism of Evil*, (San Francisco: Harper & Row, 1967), p. 233.
2. Gerhard von Rad, *Genesis*, The Old Testament Library, G. Ernest Wright et al Eds, (Philadelphia: Westminster Press & London: SCM Press, 1972), p.87.
3. Walter Brueggemann, "Genesis, Interpretation" in *A Bible Commentary for Teaching and Preaching*, James Mays et al Eds, (Atlanta: John Knox Press, 1982), p. 47.
4. Brueggemann, p. 42.
5. Phyllis Trible, *God and the Rhetoric of Sexuality*, (Philadelphia: Fortress Press, 1978), p. 128.
6. Trible, p. 85.
7. Ricoeur, p. 233.
8. Ricoeur, p.233.
9. Ricoeur, p. 252.
10. Paul Ricoeur, *The Conflict of Interpretations*, (Evanston: North-western University Press, 1974), p. 284.
11. C.H. Dodd, *The Bible Today*, (Cambridge, England: University Press, 1968), p. 113, quoted in Ricoeur, *The Conflict of Interpretations*, p. 284.
12. Erich Fromm, *You Shall Be As Gods*, (Greenwich: Fawcett Publications, 1966), p. 96.
13. Stephen Duffy, "Our Hearts of Darkness: Original Sin Revisited", *Theological Studies*, 49, (1988), p. 614.
14. Fromm, p. 22.

15. D. Solle/S. Cloyes, *To Work and to Love: A Theology of Creation* (Philadelphia: Fortress Press, 1984), p. 74.
16. Duffy, p. 614.
17. Duffy, pp. 611-614.
18. Sigmund Freud, *Introductory Lectures on Psychoanalysis,* Vol 1, (Penguin Books edition, 1978); Otto Rank, *Trauma of Birth,* (London: Routledge & Kegan Paul, 1926).
19. Erich Neumann, *Depth Psychology and the New Ethic,* (San Francisco: Harper & Row, 1972), p. 147.
20. Neumann, p. 147.
21. Fromm, p. 70.
22. Richard G. Cote, *Universal Grace: Myth or Reality,* (New York: Orbis Books, 1977), p. 32.
23. Cote, p.32.
24. Jeremy Rifken, *Declaration of a Heretic* (Boston: Routledge & Kegan Paul, 1988), pp. 109-110.
25. Duffy, p. 619.
26. Duffy, p. 598.
27. Matthew L. Lamb, "The Social and Political Dimensions of Lonergan's Theology", in *The Desires of the Human Heart: An Introduction to the Theology of Bernard Lonergan,* Vernon Gregson Ed, (New York: Paulist Press, 1988), p. 278.
28. Quoted in Lamb, p. 208.
29. Quoted in Lamb, p. 208.
30. Paul Ricoeur, *Freud and Philosophy,* pp. 32-36.

11. Widowhood Practice in some Southern Nigerian Ethnic Groups: An Appraisal

Daniel I. Ilega
University of Port Harcourt

There is no doubt as Oloko, 1997:1 says that all enduring marriages ultimately end with the death of either the husband or the wife or both but the disorganizing or traumatic experience which accompanies the death of the husband tends to be greater than that which accompanies the death of the wife. Death is at the end and it marks the beginning of religious traditions concerned with what must befall the wife or widow who lost her husband or husband who lost his wife. The treatment of the corpse starts immediately after death and may not end until after funeral and beyond depending upon the religious traditions of each society. Admittedly the widow in all known religious traditions of the world, undergoes more strenuous rites than the widower. The widows are saddled with rites which women mainly have seen as very arduous, dehumanizing and degrading whose intensity vary in different parts of the world. Women generally claim that the widowhood rites violate some of the human rights of widows and erode their self-esteem. Oloko, 1997:1, also decry the deprivative measures when it comes to the issue of inheritance. In traditional Africa, as well as in Southern Nigeria, the practice is prevalent just as women have not ceased to condemn it with whatever language they could muster.

This paper is set to show what widowhood is in some Southern Nigerian ethnic groups, its said necessity in our society, why it has to persist and how far social factors are naturally reducing what use to be its severity. This paper will also demonstrate the tradition of inheritance within studied cases, which troubles widowhood. This choice ensures not only a good coverage of our topic, but also captures what can be described as much similarities with many parts of African Society. For us, traditional Africa as a whole is a religious Society and this should call for a little treatment of what is religion. We need this knowledge because African culture, beliefs and practices, widowhood inclusive, are indisputable predicates of religion. A foreign scholar in Igboland of Southern Nigerian had no qualms in saying that the Igbos (Ejizu, 1986:154) "eat, drinks, bath, dress, sin religiously and the religion of these natives... is their existence and their existence is their religion". Idowu 1962:5 was not saying any thing different when he said the "Yorubas are in all things religions". As far as the Africans are concerned death does not write end rather it opens up a level of spiritual existence in which the dead relate with the living. Their ancestors require that the norms of society are kept and are also required to go to any length of obedience to keep the religious traditions under which widowhood must be seen to be done to prove purposes.

What is Religion and what is African Traditional Religion?

I want to think that this paper is being addressed mainly to those readers who are acquainted with religion and I may not need to tie them down to questions like what is religion and what is African traditional religion. Nevertheless, this paper will go beyond my conceived readers into the wider society. The need, however, little, can then arise to consider the questions already raised. The attempt is made to lay a religious foundation so crucial to our topic.

Religion is one of the most slippery words in the dictionary because it is difficult to define. Many scholars, both in religion and in other disciplines related and unrelated to religion, would agree that it has not yet been adequately defined. The difficulty comes from the fact that religion covers a variety of customs, beliefs and ideas so that no single definition would explain all of them. But broadly speaking, whatever else it may be seen to be, religion springs from the belief that over and above the present world in which we live, move and have our existence, there is another order of existence of some kind which influences life on earth and its inhabitants. In Southern Nigeria as elsewhere, this belief is ever made alive by individual claims of revelation from and personal contact with the beings of that order of existence.

In African Traditional Religion we talk about the Supreme Being who created the heavens and the earth and all good things, visible and invisible, and the relationship between the creator and man. In Africa, religion again, is the action between the Supreme Being, divinities, spirits, ancestors and man. Creation is however, attributed to the Supreme Being. (Robin Horton, 1983:46) has clearly observed from a cross-section of West Africa, and what can be applied elsewhere that to the Africans, the world as a whole was created and ultimately sustained by God. The understanding here is that from beginning to the end, man is in the hands of God and man stands obliged to worship God. The African, like every other person, is conscious of this obligation and this explain why in no field of activity has man expended so much time, thought, effort and even life as in the pursuit of religious goals. Consequently, man's belief resulting in complete submission of his will to the divine world in all departments of life has found expression in sacred actions or rites such as widowhood practices, the subject matter of this paper. His religious belief is answerable to his attitude to life.

There is a fact we need not be in a hurry to dispute, and that is that the African man and his indigenous religion believes and accepts that socio/political religious authority (Ilega, 1989:3) come not from men but from God and the spirits dwelling in the supersensible world. This belief is rooted in the fact that laws, culture, tribal customs, social and ritual organisations and norms of society have been ordained by the ancestors and heroes of the tribe long ago before they left the earth and retired to the outer world.

Widowhood
Widowhood, in which the wife of a dead husband is subjected to some mourning and burial rituals, is a universal phenomenon. Also universal, this seems a coincidence, is the far too less subjection of a husband whose wife is dead to mourning and burial rituals. As (Amadiume, 1987:81) who looked at widowhood in Igbo traditional society said, hardly any taboo surrounded a man's mourning for his dead wife. A man is said only to have feared possible accusations of maltreatment or murder, founded or unfounded by his deceased wife's group or relations or the community. In the Rivers State where this writer has exercised himself in this matter, the widower is permitted by the traditions of the society to do very little of mourning. (Dikibo 2001:127) claims that in Okrika a man who lost his wife is never subjected to

what he calls dehumanizing treatment even when it is obvious that he contributed to the death of his wife may be by not taking good care of her or even by beating her up or any kind of maltreatment in her life time. The man can remarry as early as he could since he could stop mourning shortly after the burial of his wife. To show some visible concern the man may shave his head and put on black dress. We will now turn to specific ethnic groups to see its pervasiveness.

Widowhood Rites among some Nigerian Ethnic Groups
A good example that could go for a documentary of how widows are treated among the Igbos of South-eastern Nigeria, has been given by Nwanna Nzewunwa, 1997:97. We must be indebted to her for our much use of the Igbo picture of widowhood practices in Igboland. We shall find that there is nothing in the Igbo treatment that cannot be replicated elsewhere in the African traditional society. Here the treatment is described as an ordeal – an activity that begins as soon as the husband dies. The woman, as in many African traditional society, becomes unclean as a result of the death. The widow must not touch anyone or be touched by anyone who is not a widow. (Howells, 1962:160) shows from his studies in New Guinea that the belief that the ghost of the husband was around puts her in a taboo state making her dangerous to other people. In the case of the Igbos the

woman becomes unclean, impure and a source of ill-luck as soon as the death of her husband is announced. As Nwanna-Nzewumum stressed to further shield the people, including her children, if any, from her contaminated situation,

> ... she was given a stick to use for scratching the body when necessary as her hands were impure, therefore cannot be used for scratching her body... She was not to talk to men, greet anybody in the morning or respond to greetings. Her children were taken away from her ... she was not allowed to have her bath for 28 days.

As someone that evil days have fallen, she is subjected to other traditional mandatory ritual requirements to fulfill. She must be moved from the husband's house to a little hut where she must pass her day and night sleeping on a mat or discarded wooden door covered with an old warn out wrapper. From the day the husband died to the day of his burial the widow is monitored to keep the rites connected with widowhood.

The "ordeal" runs full circle when burial funeral commences. As someone being "punished" unduly, she is forced to drink water used for bathing the corpse as well as sleeping with the corpse on the same bed for some hours or the whole night in a locked room. Besides what we have stated, the widow must not sleep on the night before the burial. After the burial of the husband the widow is taken to the backyard for hair shaving. The widow's mourning period which could last for a year or more is also saddled with dos and don'ts which would include a ban on her not to have relationship with any man. If this happens and she becomes pregnant the society, particularly the husband's relation, might accuse her and the encroaching man of complicity to kill the husband. The repercussion is usually there and severe. Just before we leave the Igbo society, we must state in clear terms that widowhood is mainly practiced by those who are legally married according to the traditions and customs of the people concerned. A widow may, especially if there is an issue from the marriage, inherit her husband's property and land. Tradition also makes provision for an elder male member of the dead husband to take care of the children. A childless widow, depending upon her relationship with the husband and his people, may remain with the family to remarry into it or is sent back to her parents. As we leave the Igbo land, we must drop the hint that some variations in the treatment of widows can be seen based on status of a widow.

In Rivers State where this writer could have access to on the spot happenings, one finds differences in the treatment of widows. In Okirika, according to Dikibo, 2001:129, the widow is confined in her kitchen for 5 days but could be allowed to go to the waterfront or in the sea front to bath but under escort of elder women who are widows. She must not, like in the Igbo religious tradition, greet or accept greeting from anyone, especially the men. At the end of 5 days, an elder widow would shave her hair wherever hair can be found and bury same in the mud. The elder woman would on behalf of the widow pour libation to the widow's late husband. A calabash is broken on the spot of the libation marking a complete separation for the two. The widow will remain in the late husband's house and if she is young she could have affairs with a man of her choice outside her husband's lineage. Should there be children from that love-making, the children belong to her late husband, whose property she is. Once a marriage is legal the children of the union are legitimate children and are to inherit what the father left behind.

Ofuru 2000:51 reports from Ikot Ekpene in Akwa Ibom State of Nigeria and others on how widows are treated there. According to her the moment a husband dies, his wife is immediately summoned by a group of old women who would confine her to a room, where she is forced to sit on the floor for as long as the dead is not buried. This will be followed by the shaving of her hair to the scalp. Her movement is restricted. She is not to wear shoes, sandals or slippers. She is not also allowed to cut her nails or change her dress. Above all, she is not allowed to have her bath no matter how long she is under confinement, except during her menstrual period. Even at that she has to be supervised by the same old women who had led her into confinement. However, the widow gets a little relief when the burial of her husband is concluded, for she can now change her dress and the new dress must be black. This is followed by a second hair shaving and cutting of her nails, which signify the complete separation with the dead. The next stage is to choose a husband who must be in the extended family of the dead husband. Widow and children also inherit whatever is left behind. A childless widow may be sent to her parents with little or nothing.

Among the Benin people, a widow's traditional mourning period begins on the night of the burial. The widow is taken to the back room where for the next send days she would sit on a few leaves, dry or wet on the floor as mat, next to a fire that must burn non-stop for the whole period. She is clad in a small cloth with a bundle of broomsticks in her right hand while eating with her left hand; which must remain unwashed for seven days of the funeral. The broomsticks is to ward off the spirit of the dead husband.

At dust and dawn, she goes to the back house to wail at the loss of her husband, an indication of how much she missed him. On the seventh and last day of the funeral, she keeps an all night vigil along with her relations. At about 4 am of the seventh day, she gathers her leaves, the wood and ashes from the fire, goes to a designated place which is quite some distance away from the house, and throws away all the items she used for mourning including the small cloth she had been tying. She will then return home naked, chanting songs. At home she takes her bath, ties another wrapper before entering the home. Thereafter she wears black for at least a year and does not step outside the compound for three months. As part of the funeral rites, she is compelled to drink of the water used in washing the corpse, thereby swearing that she had in no way contributed to her husband's death.

A good work on the Ikwerre widowhood institution has been done by Ofuru, 2000: We want to present views from this work. It is a study specifically on Elele Alimini Community in Ikwerre land. In Ikwerre communities, there may be significant differences from place to place. At the death of a husband the widow is immediately confined to a room by the daughters of the land. They are mainly of the husband's family; married or unmarried. The widow is made to sit on a mat or a small kitchen stool for two or three weeks. The widow then undergoes an oath of innocence. In this case, she is compelled by tradition to drink of the water used in washing the husband's corpse. The belief is that if her hand is clean (innocent), no evil thing will come her way throughout her mourning period. Thus if no serious sickness or death befalls her, within the mourning period then she has proved her innocence. However, if within this period she dies, it will then be assumed by all the community people that, she was responsible for her husband's death. The belief is that her late husband has avenged his death by taking her along. In this case the widow is tied with a mat and thrown into the evil forest without any one whatsoever weeping over her death. Hence again, I must state that the tradition does not give room for accident. The common belief in Elele Alimini about the tradition is that the gods will not allow her to die while mourning her husband. Again, as in other Ikwerre communities, a widow in Elele Alimini is never allowed to cook her meals until after the burial of her husband because cooking, as we all know is a source of joy, and because the husband will not partake in eating the meal.

Another reason why she is not allowed to cook her meals is due to the situation at hand (the death of her husband). All her meals and those of her entire household have to be prepared by other widows or her relatives and friends. As in most traditions we have surveyed, the Ikwerre widow must not only cry aloud all day but also shave off her hair and wear mourning appearance and be clad in black dresses.

So far we have treated very selectively widowhood practices in some areas around our place of writing namely, Southern Nigeria. We have been so restrictive because a survey of widowhood in African society will show more of similarities than dissimilarity.

Overview of the Treatments

Are the treatments unjust, oppressive, wicked and dehumanizing? The women think so and believe that men are responsible for denying them equal opportunity with them. Men are also accused of gender discrimination and subjugation. Several conferences have been held by women in many nations to ask for equality with men in all departments. Concerning widowhood rituals, the women are of the opinion that men can as well bear as much as they have been made to bear.

In *Today's Women*, 1975, the year 1975 was designated international women's year by the United Nations to focus world attention on the status of women, their rights and responsibilities. Among the goals drawn up was that of promoting equality between men and women. In some write ups in newspapers, journals, magazines etc, this issue of equality is banged about as if they have forgotten that God and traditions of the world made them weaker vessels to be protected by men. Specifically on widowhood practice, women tend to blame their fellow women for obeying the religious traditions even as we know that disobedience could create social chaos. In their quest for freedom on all fronts, they believe it is their rights to even choose when to get pregnant and when to put a halt to childbearing. This kind of freedom will not help women, it can create problems to marriage. They are not being punished when they are asked to obey widowhood rituals but to fulfill the traditions. The traditional rituals are consumable products. They come and go and they go back to normal.

Some Reasons for the Practice
Here, in Africa, the belief is strong and common that death marks the empowerment of the dead. In order words, a dead person has much power that can be used to deal with the living. They can revenge evil for evil or good for good. After words it is the dead husband who is believed to be the ancestor-a link between the dead and the living. The dead expect their family members to find out what killed them and possibly avenge their death. When the death of a husband occurs, the wife is the prime suspect. As (Oloko, 1997:1) made clear, " it is believed that a woman could eliminate her husband out of jealousy for her husband overt or covert polygamy". Besides, witchcraft accusations are spread about after any death in Africa. Wives were usually accused of using witchcraft to kill their husband. While Sarah Oloko has her own bitterness against "harsh" treatment of widows, she could afford to say that

> *The spirit of the husband is likely to hover around his widow with whom he had the greatest intimacy during his life time, ritual cleansing are needed to sever the attachment between the husband and wife. The more unattractive the woman is made in the process of ritual cleansing the more she is both to the spirit of her husband and intending lovers or suitors.*

It is the opinion of Sarah, a candid opinion in deed, that the harsh circumstances of widows are perceived in the communities which perpetrate the difficult circumstances as "well-intention acts which evolved traditionally to protect the living from the dead". Widowhood at different levels of acts, in traditional African society should be seen on its merit as a protective institution. It has even become impossible for Christianity and Islam to eliminate it because widowhood rituals form an essential part of traditional burial rites. It is also clear that education, an essential element of change in Africa, has not been able to do much beyond reducing the rites among women in urban centers. Widows who are in urban centers can hardly be tied down to the long days, of ritual mourning especially when they are in government or private jobs. The main victims are those in the rural areas though the religions are educating them to regard the rituals as idolatry. Again, widows with illiterate in-laws are likely to suffer more than widows with educationally enlightened in-laws.

Some women, if we can add, easily understand Widowhood practice, as a necessary but ugly period a widow has to pass through. Ofuru, 2000:55 quoted a Benin woman to have offered that.

> *The treatment, though it looks bad, is a stage which a widow passes through in the kingdom of Benin. It is not a permanent feature of Benin widow and should not be seen or decried as punishment against women. The mourning period of a widow is a religious tradition.*

In the same vein (Nwanna-Nzewunwa, 101) saw clearly the need for this institution when she said that.

> *Widowhood practices in Igboland were adopted with a view to satisfying the varied requirements of the dead (ancestors and spirits) and his living kinsmen and members of his community.*

This paper is supporting the various views we have expressed here that widowhood institution is not only necessary but that the rituals are just for a brief period in the life of a widow. Even then the paper would advocate moderation.

Nzewunwa says that in Igbo tradition when a person dies, the cause must be established. This is true because everyone is a suspect when death occurs and every one is anxious to pull himself or herself out of the accusations, no matter what they go through. Widows, as we have mentioned already, are the core suspects, and the only way for them to set themselves free, if innocent, is to prepare for whatever measures traditions have set up. If we can repeat, widowhood rituals are established for a purpose in African society. It is true that the practice hurts the flesh, but the widow comes out fresh and acceptable to society.

An Appraisal
The keen reader will not miss knowing what we have been saying concerning widowhood practices in African traditional society. We may be saying just the same thing in this endnote in different use of words. We have declined to see the treatments as unjust even as we see them harsh. Sometimes the police need to be harsh to elicit truth from accused. The severe part of widowhood ritual will not remain forever but like human sacrifice and twins killing in ancient Africa, may one day be phased out. And the gods would oblige.

Religion is dynamic not static and with education, especially when the widow is on the job, days of confinement indoors have been shortened and may continue to be so. Nwanna-Nzewunnwa made this point for the Igbo society as she wrote that the more educated and enlightened widows know their rights in inheritance, an issue we did not give sectional devotion, but interjected here and there, the more the rites are gradually been mellowed down.

Islam and Christianity, though appear helpless in totally stopping the practice, is another area where widowhood rites are being disorganized. Christian and Muslim women disregard most of the practices as the practices are seen as contrary to their beliefs. Most widows these days cannot, for example, be forced to marry the relations of their dead husbands. With the ever spreading of two of the three main African religions into rural Africa those who leave the way of their fathers are very likely to disown the rituals. Widowhood practice as obvious, especially in urban Africa, will one day be consigned to only mourning and wearing of mourning dresses. Accusations may continue but the ancestors will deal with offenders in new ways short of harshness, confinement etc. As more and more people get conscious of the divine instruction in the Bible, as found in Exodus 22, that widows should not be maltreated, more tolerance would be seen in dealing with widowhood practices.

References

Amadiume, *Ify Male Daughters, Female Husband Gender and Sex in an African Society*, Zed Books London, 1987.

Dikibo, A.P. *"Language, Culture and Personality*: A Survey of Marriage and Widowhood in Okrika", in Historical and Cultural Perspectives of Rivers State, Aminiphilips (ed.) ISCAP Enterprises, Port Harcourt, 2001.

Ejizu, C. "Continuity and Discontinuity in Igbo Traditional Religion" in Ikenga-Metuh, (ed.). The Gods in Retreat, Fourth Dimension Publishers, Enugu, 1986.

Horton, R. "African and Western Social Psychologies "in Meyer Fortes Oedipus and Job in West African Religion, Cambridge Social Anthropology, Cambridge University Press, London, 1983.

Howells, W. The Heathens: Primitive Man and his Religion. Doubleday, New York, 1962.

Ilega, D.I. "The Indispensability of Religion to Politics in African Traditions" *The Nigerian Ecclesiastical Journal*, Vol. 1 No. 3

Nwanna-Nzewunwa, O.P. Widowhood Practices in Igbo Culture: A Sociological Analysis, *Nigerian Journal of Professional Studies in Education*, University of Port Harcourt, Vol. 5, 1997.

Ofuru, H.C. Widowhood in Elele-Alimini: A Socio-Religious Analysis. Unpublished M. A. Thesis University of Port Harcourt, 2000.

Oloko, S.B. A Panoramic View of Widowhood in Nigeria, Department of Educational Foundation, University of Lagos Publication. 1997.

Today's Woman, 1975 Publication.

www.ingramcontent.com/pod-product-compliance
Lightning Source LLC
Chambersburg PA
CBHW070827300426
44111CB00014B/2477